THE INDIAN MINIBIKE SAGA – with help from Wikipedia

During the 1960s, Floyd Clymer 'assumed' ownership of the Indian Motorcycle Company name, apparently without purchasing it from the legitimate trademark holder.

In 1968 he entered into a partnership arrangement with Italjet, a motorcycle manufacturer based in Italy. He commissioned Italian ex-pilot and engineer Leopoldo Tartarini, owner of Italjet Moto, to manufacture Minarelli-engined 50 cc minibikes using the Indian name.

Unfortunately, Floyd's untimely death in January 1970 ended his attempt to revive the Indian marque. However, after Clymer's death his widow sold the alleged Indian trademark to Los Angeles attorney Alan Newman, who continued to import minibikes made by Italjet, and later manufactured in a wholly owned assembly plant located in Taipei (Taiwan). Several models with engine displacement between 50 cc and 175 cc were produced, mostly fitted with Italian two-stroke engines made either by Italjet or Franco Morini, but the fortunes of this venture didn't last long. By 1975, sales were dwindling, and in January 1977, the company was declared bankrupt.

An illustrated parts list for the Clymer 50 cc Ponybike, Boy Racer and Papoose minibikes was a necessity for the network of dealers that Clymer envisioned and it was obviously intended to be a 'dealer only' publication. However, it is also apparent that the parts list published by Clymer was culled from the Italjet documentation appropriately modified for the Indian minibikes. As a result the Clymer parts list is probably the rarest of all the Floyd Clymer Publications. It is rare for a number of reasons, not the least of which is the fact that his involvement with the Italjet Indian minibikes was sill in the fledgling stage at the time of his death. In addition, as Floyd had only imported a small number of these 50cc minibikes there was little justification in printing large quantities of this 'dealer only' publication. .

This illustrated parts list is a valuable reference for any Ponybike, Boy Racer and Papoose minibike owner and a 'must have' resource for any Clymer, Italjet, and Indian minibike enthusiast. The exploded diagrams in the parts list would be a critical part of any restoration project and the addition of a selection of photographs, reviews and data sheets for the various models from Clymer's original sales literature makes for easy identification of original construction details.

The original parts list was comb bound with card covers and was printed on euro sized 'foolscap' paper and some minor re-sizing was required - otherwise this is a faithful reproduction of the original. This truly scarce publication is almost impossible to find on the secondary market and we are pleased to be able to offer this reproduction as a service to all Clymer, Italjet, Indian minibike owners and enthusiasts worldwide.

WWW.VELOCEPRESS.COM

PONYBIKE

Sales Literature Scrap Book Pages 3 to 11

Illustrated Parts List Pages 13 to 39

Indian: PONYBIKE AND PAPOOSE

One little, two little fifties from the Clymer-Munch tribe...

ONE LITTLE, two little... Ah, it's well known that there exist Zuni, Arapaho, Yavapi and Umatilla. But, Clymer-Munch is a relative newcomer among the names on the tribal roll. And, Papoose and Ponybike are the braves of that latter tribe.

Floyd Clymer, long-time two-wheel entrepeneur, Freidel Munch, West Germany's Mammothman, and assorted British, Italian and Czechoslovakian representatives of manufacturers of proprietary motorcycle, moped and minibike components have commingled to produce machinery, escalating from 50 cc, through mid-range displacements, to the mammoth 1000-cc Mammoth. The 50-cc segment includes the aforementioned Papoose and Ponybike.

This pair of machines can be classed as belonging to one of two categories—small, vest pocket motorcycle, or large, overdressed minibike. Both are distributed through franchised dealers by Floyd Clymer's Motorcycle Division, Los Angeles, Calif.

The Ponybike and Papoose share a number of features. Both are equipped with telescopic forks and swinging arm rear suspension; both are equipped with

full (magneto type) lighting; both are fitted with internal expanding brakes, front and rear. Beyond this, the similarities become a bit broader, and outright differences begin to appear.

The Ponybike is based on a single truss frame. The 50-cc Jawa/CZ two-stroke engine is suspended beneath this single downtube from a pair of welded-on plates, stamped deeply for stiffening. The Czech powerplant, on 9:1 compression, develops 4.8 bhp at 8000 rpm. Power is delivered through a gear primary drive, through a three-speed gearbox and multi-disc wet clutch, to a single-row chain final drive.

The Papoose, on the other hand, is powered by a B.F. Minarelli engine of 49.6-cc piston displacement and 10:1 compression. Likewise, the 4.19-bhp engine, which also peaks at 8000 rpm, has a gear primary drive. However, the gearbox is a four-speed unit. The Papoose's clutch also is a multi-plate, wet assembly; and, final drive is by single-row chain. The engine-gearbox is suspended from a single downtube by an inverted-U yoke arrangement.

Both engines operate on regular grade fuel, with a 20:1 oil-in-fuel mix. Both employ magneto ignition and folding crank kick starters.

The machines investigated and ridden by CYCLE WORLD crewmen both showed a degree of workmanship and attention to detail not found on the domestic minibike.

Paint on the fire engine red Papoose and the bronze, gold and white Ponybike appeared flawless.

Cables, clutch and brake levers (ball end on the Papoose, blade end on the Ponybike), lighting equipment, and handlebar grips all are recognizable as items drawn from that vast well of motorcycle components that is Italy. These things complete the slick, finished aura of the Clymer superminis, as compared with the rough welded, backyard mechanicals of the domestic product.

Performance of the Ponybike and Papoose are indistinguishable one from the other. Both approach the 50-mph mark for top speed. Both exhibit the excessively quick steering that is directly associated with small diameter wheels, though the control ratio isn't as abrupt, say, as with the 6-in. wheels of the true minibike. Both machines go well on pavement and on hard off-road surfaces. In sand, unfortunately, neither the Jawa/CZ nor the Minarelli engine is capable of sufficient torque delivery to permit continued progress. In sand, unfortunately, these machines invariably bog down to stay. The Ponybike is offered with optional block tread tires. These would do little, without sufficient power to make the added traction worthwhile.

List price of either machine is in the $300 bracket—something more than the average minibike, something less than the average motorcycle, which is what the Papoose or Ponybike buyer expects for his money. And, this purchaser, in addition to acquiring one of the cutest of the sub-motorcycle range, also will acquire title to that once-magic, ever-nostalgic name, Indian.

INDIAN PONYBIKE
This unique road or trail bike has 3 speeds, 5 H.P., 45-48 mph. Full suspension front and rear. Dual seat, road or trail tires. 2 brakes, lites. Red or blue. A **large** minibike. Immediate delivery. **$295**

Ponybike weighs 100 lbs.,
Mammoth 540 lbs.
Quite a contrast.

Standing directly back of the Indian Ponybike is world-renowned motorcycle stylist, engineer and designer, Leopold Tatarini, a former Italian racing champion. Others in the photo, L to R, are Indian manufacturer, Floyd Clymer, and students, Michele Ferrandio and Monica Martello.

A portion of a day's production of Indian Ponybikes ready for crating and shipment to the United States.

Side view of Ponybike

Front view of Ponybike

Linda Vaughn, the famous Miss Hurst, on Ponybike. She is publicity girl for Hurst race and stock car products.

These photos, taken at the factory, show one-half of the first shipment of Indian Ponybikes to the United States. The machines are assembled on the slowly moving chain asembly line at the left. The finished units are now ready for crating for U.S. shipment.

FAMOUS INDIANAPOLIS "500" RACE PERSONALITIES ON INDIANS

Upper left – one of Indy all-time greats, 3-time winner Mauri Rose, on Ponybike. Below – Mauri rides down pit area where he stopped many times in his racing days. Lower right-Harlan Fengler, veteran race driver and "500" Stewart on Ponybike. Upper right–Indy track owner, Tony Hulman. Tony in his University of Indiana days, owned and raced Indians on half-mile dirt tracks in Indiana. He tells Floyd Clymer, "It's good to see Indian back again. I can remember when Indian was No 1 in U.S. sales." Tony also has several old Indians in the Speedway Museum, including the Indian once raced by famous Cannonball Baker.

Indian: PONYBIKE AND PAPOOSE
One little, two little fifties from the Clymer-Munch tribe

ONE LITTLE, two little... Ah, it's well known that there exist Zuni, Arapaho, Yavapi and Umatilla. But, Clymer-Munch is a relative newcomer among the names on the tribal roll. And, Papoose and Ponybike are the braves of that latter tribe.

This pair of machines can be classed as belonging to one of two categories—small, vest pocket motorcycle, or large, overdressed minibike. Both are distributed through franchised dealers by Floyd Clymer's Motorcycle Division, Los Angeles, Calif.

The Ponybike and Papoose share a number of features. Both are equipped with telescopic forks and swinging arm rear suspension; both are equipped with full (magneto type) lighting; both are fitted with internal expanding brakes, front and rear. Beyond this, the similarities become a bit broader, and outright differences begin to appear.

The Ponybike is based on a single truss frame. The 50-cc Jawa/CZ two-stroke engine is suspended beneath this single downtube from a pair of welded-on plates, stamped deeply for stiffening. The Czech powerplant, on 9:1 compression, develops 4.8 bhp at 8000 rpm. Power is delivered through a gear primary drive, through a three-speed gearbox and multi-disc wet clutch, to a single-row chain final drive.

The Papoose, on the other hand, is powered by a B.F. Minarelli engine of 49.6-cc piston displacement and 10:1 compression. Likewise, the 4.19-bhp engine, which also peaks at 8000 rpm, has a gear primary drive. However, the gearbox is a four-speed unit. The Papoose's clutch also is a multi-plate, wet assembly; and, final drive is by single-row chain. The engine-gearbox is suspended from a single downtube by an inverted-U yoke arrangement.

Both engines operate on regular grade fuel, with a 20:1 oil-in-fuel mix. Both employ magneto ignition and folding crank kick starters.

The machines investigated and ridden by CYCLE WORLD crewmen both showed a degree of workmanship and attention to detail not found on the domestic minibike.

Paint on the fire engine red Papoose and the bronze, gold and white Ponybike appeared flawless.

Cables, clutch and brake levers (ball end on the Papoose, blade end on the Ponybike), lighting equipment, and handlebar grips all are recognizable as items drawn from that vast well of motorcycle components that is Italy. These things complete the slick, finished aura of the Clymer superminis, as compared with the rough welded, backyard mechanicals of the domestic product.

Performance of the Ponybike and Papoose are indistinguishable one from the other. Both approach the 50-mph mark for top speed. Both exhibit the excessively quick steering that is directly associated with small diameter wheels, though the control ratio isn't as abrupt, say, as with the 6-in. wheels of the true minibike. Both machines go well on pavement and on hard off-road surfaces. In sand, unfortunately, neither the Jawa/CZ nor the Minarelli engine is capable of sufficient torque delivery to permit continued progress. In sand, unfortunately, these machines invariably bog down to stay. The Ponybike is offered with optional block tread tires. These would do little, without sufficient power to make the added traction worthwhile.

List price of either machine is in the $300 bracket—something more than the average minibike, something less than the average motorcycle, which is what the Papoose or Ponybike buyer expects for his money. And, this purchaser, in addition to acquiring one of the cutest of the sub-motorcycle range, also will acquire title to that once-magic, ever-nostalgic name, Indian.

INDIAN PONYBIKE

INDIAN PAPOOSE

A portion of a day's production of Indian Pony-bikes ready for crating and shipment to the United States.

DEALERS — We have an attractive proposition. If you want a unique line $295 to $4,000, we have them. Get **plus** business, full profit due to demand exceeding supply. Write for details.

Send for full details and brochure.
FLOYD CLYMER
MOTORCYCLE DIVISION

222 N. VIRGIL AVE.,
LOS ANGELES, CALIF. 90004
TEL.: (213) 388-5119

FLOYD CLYMER MOTORCYCLE DIVISION

222 N. Virgil Avenue • Los Angeles, California 90004
Phone: (213) 388-5119 • Cable: "Clymer" Los Angeles

MANUFACTURERS
Indian Motorcycles made in Italy
•
U.S. and Canadian distributors for
Clymer-Minarelli
cycle and minibike 2-stroke engines
and
Clymer-Tartarini Telescopic Forks
and
Royal-Enfield British Motorcycles
for all states west of Mississippi River

IMPORTANT NOTICE
SPECIAL OFFER!

These INDIANS are stylish, well designed and engineered, and beautifully finished with excellent paint jobs. They are actually small motorcycles or super (large) minibikes, yet small enough to fit easily into a station wagon, passenger car trunk (if handlebars are lowered), camper, truck, airplane, boat or mobile home.

Easier to ride and SAFER - They are easier riding and SAFER than most minibikes because they have speeds up to 50 mph, with a 2-stroke 50cc engine that performs more like a 90cc than a 50. Two brakes, front and rear, and full spring suspension make for E-Z riding and handling as they have wire spoke wheels and Pirelli tires (10 x 3.00 front, 10 x 3.50 rear - larger than most minibikes).

INDIAN, the oldest name in U. S. motorcycling, offers the following features, many of them exclusive, on these models:

PAPOOSE -- 4-speed, 50 mph, the best of our minis! Price is $345.00 F.O.B. Los Angeles, crated ready to ship, with regular road tires. Dual seat. Add $10.00 per wheel if you want knobby (trail) tires. Specify red or blue color.

PONYBIKE -- 3-speed, 50 mph, trail bike special. Price $295.00 crated ready to ship, with road tires and dual seat. Add $10.00 per wheel for knobby (trail) tires. Specify gold or red color.

Lights, front and rear, and speedometer included as standard equipment on Papoose and Ponybike models.

BOY RACER -- With 2.25 x 16" tires and wire spoke wheels. 50 mph. For kids 6 to 18 years of age. It's really too small for adults, as it is a real scaled down motorcycle, but not a toy. It's a practical bike. The larger-than-scooter wheels enables the rider to "broadside" on dirt corners just like a big bike. Specify red or blue color. $325.00. Add $10.00 per wheel if you want knobby (trail) tires. Has no lights or speedo, as it is strictly an off-the-road model.

INFORMATION ON ABOVE BIKES --

PRICES -- are F.O.B. our Los Angeles warehouse. Includes delivery to airport or freight office (either motor truck or rail).

World's Largest Publisher of Books on Autos, Motorcycles, Racing and Americana

SHIPPED COMPLETE -- Not in knocked down kit form. Packed one to a crate.
Easy to set up. Only necessary to uncrate, attach handlebars and footpegs
(about 20 minutes work), add mixture of regular gas and oil and you are
ready to roll.

TERMS -- Cash. We have no time payment plan; however, buyer may deduct 3%
cash discount if remittance is sent with order. If machines are sent C.O.D.
or sight draft through a bank, the 3% discount does not apply - only if remittance is sent with order.

SPARE PARTS -- We have large stocks in Los Angeles. Almost overnight service
to any U. S. location.

GUARANTEE -- 30 days or 1,000 miles, whichever comes first.

APPROXIMATE SHIPPING COSTS -- Machines weigh 99 to 106 lbs. Crated about
115 lbs. Motor truck is cheapest and charges run from $4.00 to $6.00 per
machine to West Coast states (3 to 4 days arrival time); $12.00 to $14.00
to Mountain states (5 to 7 days arrival time); $15.00 to $16.00 to Midwest
states (8 to 10 days arrival time); $18.00 to $20.00 to Eastern states and
far South (12 to 14 days arrival time). You pay transportation upon arrival.

AIR SHIPMENTS - You may want air shipment, and air freight is very reasonable. Add about 50% of above estimates for air freight. Usually overnight
delivery to large cities with airports suitable for jets. Another day or so
if transfer is necessary for air or truck freight to small towns or cities
with small airports. If you are near a large city, it is best and faster if
we send directly to the airport, marked "HOLD FOR PICKUP" (example: Notify
John Doe - phone POdunk 666-8888).

For instance, we shipped a Papoose to a Pontiac dealer, marked "hold for
pickup at TWA office Pittsburgh, Pa." He drove 70 miles and had his bike
at 9:00 A.M. the following morning. It would have taken two or three more
days had it been transferred to a truck to haul 70 miles to his small town.

TITLE AND INSTRUCTIONS -- We send these by air mail when the bike is shipped.
The "Certificate of Origin" is your bill of sale, and we include a paid
invoice and instructions for setting up and operation.

Indian TECHNICAL DATA CHART

	PONYBIKE	BOY RACER	PAPOOSE
Engine:	Jawa M-20	Jawa M-20	Minarelli P4 "Sport"
Type:	Two-Stroke	Two-Stroke	Two-Stroke
No. of Cylinders:	One	One	One
Displacement:	50cc.	50cc.	50cc.
Bore:	38mm.	38mm.	38.8mm.
Stroke:	44mm.	44mm.	42mm.
Horsepower:	4.8	4.8	4.9
Compression Ratio:	8.0:1	8.0:1	9.0:1
Carburetor:	Jikov	Dellorto SHA 14.14	Dellorto UA19S
Fuel Capacity:	1.2 Gal.	1.2 Gal.	1.2 Gal.
Lubrication:	Gas/Oil Mixture	Gas/Oil Mixture	Gas/Oil Mixture
Clutch:	Multi. Disc in Oil	Multi. Disc in Oil	Multi. Disc in Oil
Primary Drive:	Chain	Chain	Helical Gear
Ignition & Lights:	Magneto, 6volt-20Watt	Magneto, 6V. - 20W.	Magneto, 6V. - 23W.
Gear Ratios: 1st	28.99:1	28.99:1	15.22:1
2nd	15.21:1	15.21:1	9.55:1
3rd	10.28:1	10.28:1	6.64:1
4th	-	-	5.30:1
Final Drive Ratio:	3.92:1	4.61:1	57:1
Tires: (Pirelli)	front-3.00 x 10	front - 2½ x 16	front - 3.00 x 10
	rear - 3.50 x 10	rear - 2½ x 16	rear - 3.00 x 10
Suspension: front:	Telescopic Fork	Telescopic Fork	Telescopic Fork
rear:	Swing Arm w/Damper	Swing Arm w/Damper	Swing Arm w/Damper
Weight: (Dry)	106 lbs.	99 lbs.	105 lbs.
Wheelbase:	42 in.	41 in.	38 in.
Ground Clearance:	7 in.	8 in.	6 in.
Foot Peg Height:	9 in.	9.5 in.	8 in.
Seat Height:	28 in.	26 in.	27 in.
Top Speed:	45 m.p.h.	50 m.p.h.	50 m.p.h.
Colors Availible:	Red, Metallic Gold	Red & White, Blue & White	Metallic Red, Metallic Blue

NOTES

| INDIAN-CLYMER MOTORCYCLE DIVISION | GROUP FRAME Refer to: (Photo No. 1   Page No. 4) | Page No 1 |

Part number	No. Pcs.	DESCRIPTION
11100	1	Frame
11103	1	Bracket
11101	1	Side stand
618	1	Spring
11102	1	Rear fork
2105	2	Bush nylon
2104	1	Pivot TE 12MBx156
10501	1	Front fork complete
10401/1	1	Fork body
10501/1	1	R.H. fork leg
10501/2	1	L.H. fork leg
10401/4	1	Plate
10401/5	2	Rubber
10401/6	2	Spring
10401/7	2	Bush nylon below
10401/8	2	Upper bush nylon
10006/6	2	Felt
10401/9	2	Plate
10006/8	2	Plate
10006/10	2	Pin
10006/11	2	Nut 8MA
10006/12	2	Washer
10401/10	2	Nut 8MA
10401/11	4	Inner washer
11104	1	Front fender inox
11105	1	Rear fender inox
10504	2	Front fender bracket
10256	2	Rear shock-absorber mm. 290
602/21	4	Spacer
11106	1	Seat
608	1	Outer upper steering column bearing
609	1	Outer lower steering column bearing

INDIAN-CLYMER MOTORCYCLE DIVISION	GROUP FRAME Refer to: (Photo No. 1 Page No. 4)	Page No 2

Part number	No. Pcs.	DESCRIPTION
610	1	Inner upper steering column bearing
611	1	Inner lower steering column bearing
613	1	Nut
613/1	2	Washer
612	52	Ball
11107	1	Chain guard
3020	2	Foot rest
8033	2	Rubber
848	1	Couple chain stretcher
10046	1	Engine
10046/1	1	Kick starter lever
11122	1	Gear change lever complete
11125	1	Filter carburettor connection
10045/1	1	Filter SHA 14/14
10045/2	1	Filter
10045/3	1	Circlip
10045/4	1	Screw
11123	1	Circlip
11108	1	Fuel tank
10042	1	Fuel tank plug
11120	1	Tank rest felt
652	1	fuel cock one way
633	1	Fuel cock two ways
634	5	Fuel cock gasket
639	1	Tool box
11109	1	Fuel connection between cocks
11109/1	1	Fuel connection cock - carburettor
11117	1	Couple Indian Clymer Tartarini decalco
11110	1	"PONYBIKE" decalco
12226	1	Decalco "designed by Tartarini"
638	1	Tool bag
11111	1	Bracket

INDIAN-CLYMER MOTORCYCLE DIVISION	GROUP FRAME Refer to: (Photo No. 1 Page No. 4)	Page No 3
Part number	No. Pcs.	DESCRIPTION
11113	1	Exhaust pipe and silencer
10066	2	Gasket
10151	1	Silencer cover
697	4	Shock-absorber spacer

page n. 4

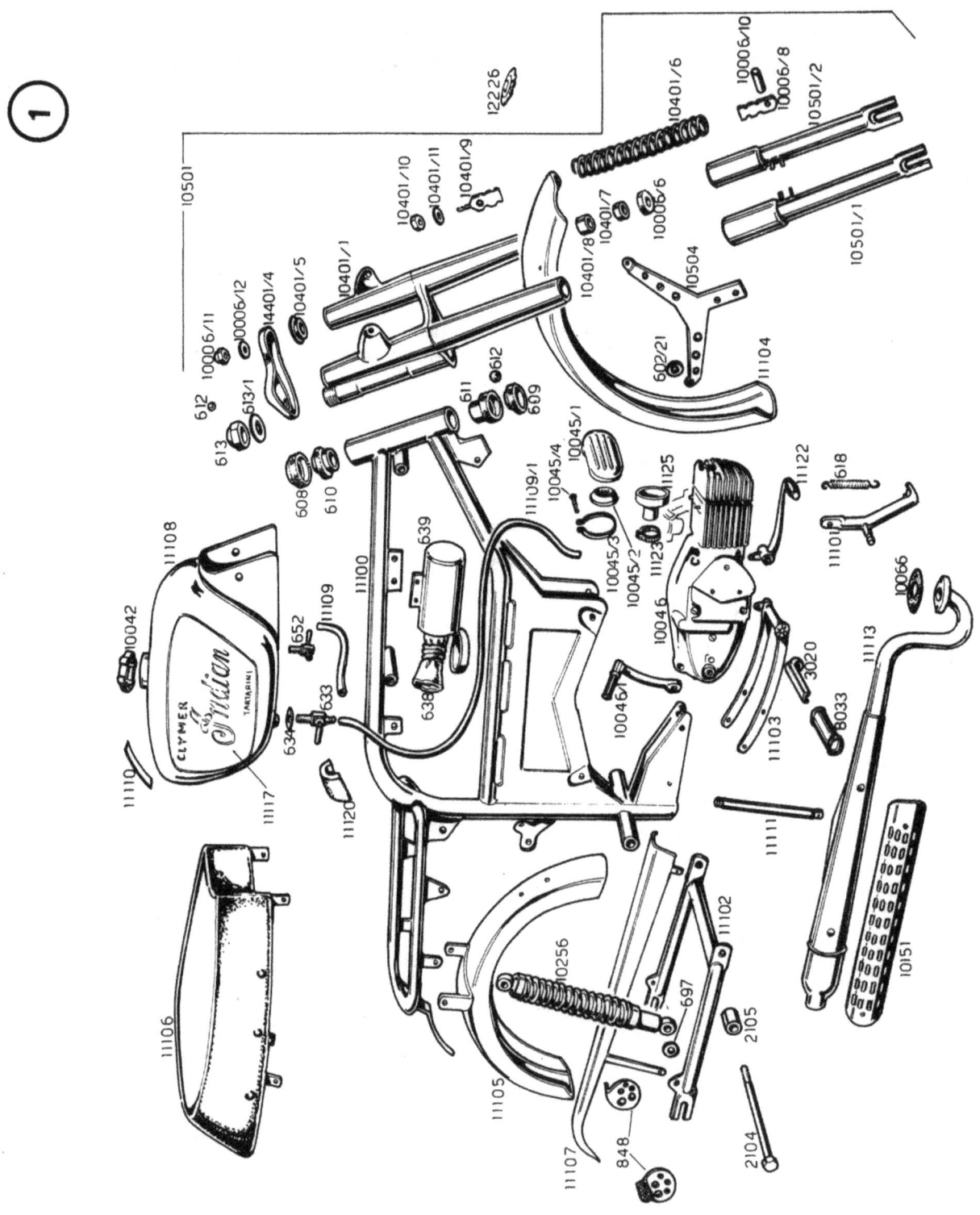

| INDIAN-CLYMER MOTORCYCLE DIVISION | GROUP
CONTROLS AND WHEELS
Refer to: (Photo No. 2   Page No. 9) | Page No 5 |

Part number	No. Pcs.	DESCRIPTION
11126	1	Handle bar
10017	1	Gas control and front brake lever without handle
10018	1	Clutch control without handle
10017/3	1	Gas control body
10017/4	1	Ring
10017/5	1	Screw
10017/1	1	Front brake lever
10017/6	2	Screw
10017/2	2	Pawl
10017/7	2	Spring
10018/2	1	Clutch control body
10018/3	1	Screw
10018/1	1	Clutch lever
1439	2	Little fork fixing handle bar
10228	1	R.H. handle
10229	1	L.H. handle
659	2	Hold-fast
10021/1	1	Wire gas control
11118	1	Wire clutch control
11119	1	Wire front brake control
10188	1	Wire rear brake control
10026	1	Tire 3.00 - 10 regular
10027	1	Tire 3.50 - 10 regular
10500	1	Tire 3.00 - 10 knobby
10043	1 or 2	Tube 9A 10
10044	1	Tube 12A 10
10028	2	Flaps
10413	1	Complete front wheel without tire
11114	1	Complete rear wheel without tire
10413/1	1	Front hub complete
10413/2	1	Front hub body
10413/3	1	Pin

INDIAN-CLYMER MOTORCYCLE DIVISION	GROUP CONTROLS AND WHEELS Refer to: (Photo No. 2 Page No. 9)	Page No. 6

Part number	No. Pcs.	DESCRIPTION
10035/3	4	Cap
10035/4	4	Cone
10035/5	4	Dust cover
10035/6	4	Nut
681/7	40	Ball
682/9	4	Nut
10413/6	1	Spacer h. 3
10413/4	1	Spacer h. 6
682/15	4	Washer
10036/3	2	Pairs of shoes with sole
10036/4	4	Spring
10036/5	2	Spinner
10036/6	2	Nut
10036/7	2	Washer
10036/8	2	Lever
10413/5	1	Cover
681/12	1	Adjuster
681/18	2	Clamp with nut and washer
10036	1	Complete rear hub
10036/1	1	Rear hub body
10036/2	1	Pin
10036/9	1	Cover
10036/10	1	Spacer h. 14
10035/7	1	Spacer
677	1	Plate
10221/4	2	Nut
682/13	4	Bolt fixing sprocket
682/14	4	Nut
10221/3	1	Tender
11114/1	1	Wheel sprocket 50T.
10032	2	Steel rim 10x54
10033	56	Nipples

INDIAN-CLYMER MOTORCYCLE DIVISION	GROUP CONTROLS AND WHEELS Refer to: (Photo No. 2 Page No. 9)	Page No 7

Part number	No. Pcs.	DESCRIPTION
10034	28	Front spoke ∅ 2,5
10221/2	28	Rear spoke ∅ 3
10050	1	Spring
10186	1	Rear brake lever
11121	1	Chain 104 links
684/1	3	Clip
684	3	Long clip
11115	1	Cables assembly
10039	1	Light switch
985/1	1	Coil cable
10052	1	Head lamp complete ∅ 105
10052/1	1	Head lamp body
10052/2	1	Head lamp ring with screw
10052/3	1	Optical set
10052/4	12	Spring
10053	1	Tail lamp with plate holder
10053/1	1	Tail lamp body
10053/2	1	Plate holder
10053/3	1	Tail lamp glass
10053/4	1	Bulb
10053/5	1	Rubber
10053/6	1	Glass gasket
10053/7	1	Cap
10053/8	1	Glass for illumination plate
10053/9	2	Screw
10053/10	2	Nut
10053/11	2	Washer
10048	1	Stop switch
10068	1	Plug pipe
11050/1	2	Clip
1440	1	Horn 6V. 18W.
11050	1	Outer ignition coil

INDIAN-CLYMER MOTORCYCLE DIVISION	GROUP CONTROLS AND WHEELS Refer to: (Photo No. 2 Page No. 9)	Page No 8

Part number	No. Pcs.	DESCRIPTION
11051	1	Plug pipe
8071	1	Cap
11116	1	Complete speedometer set
11116/1	1	Speedometer body
10227/1	1	Speedometer drive
10412/1	1	Complete cable / 550
10412/3	1	Housing cable
10412/4	1	Inner cable
3115	1	Ring
690	1	Rubber cable way
692	1	Seeger
693	2	Cables guard
10187	1	Pivot
11049	1	Cable way
10049	1	Plate

page n. 9

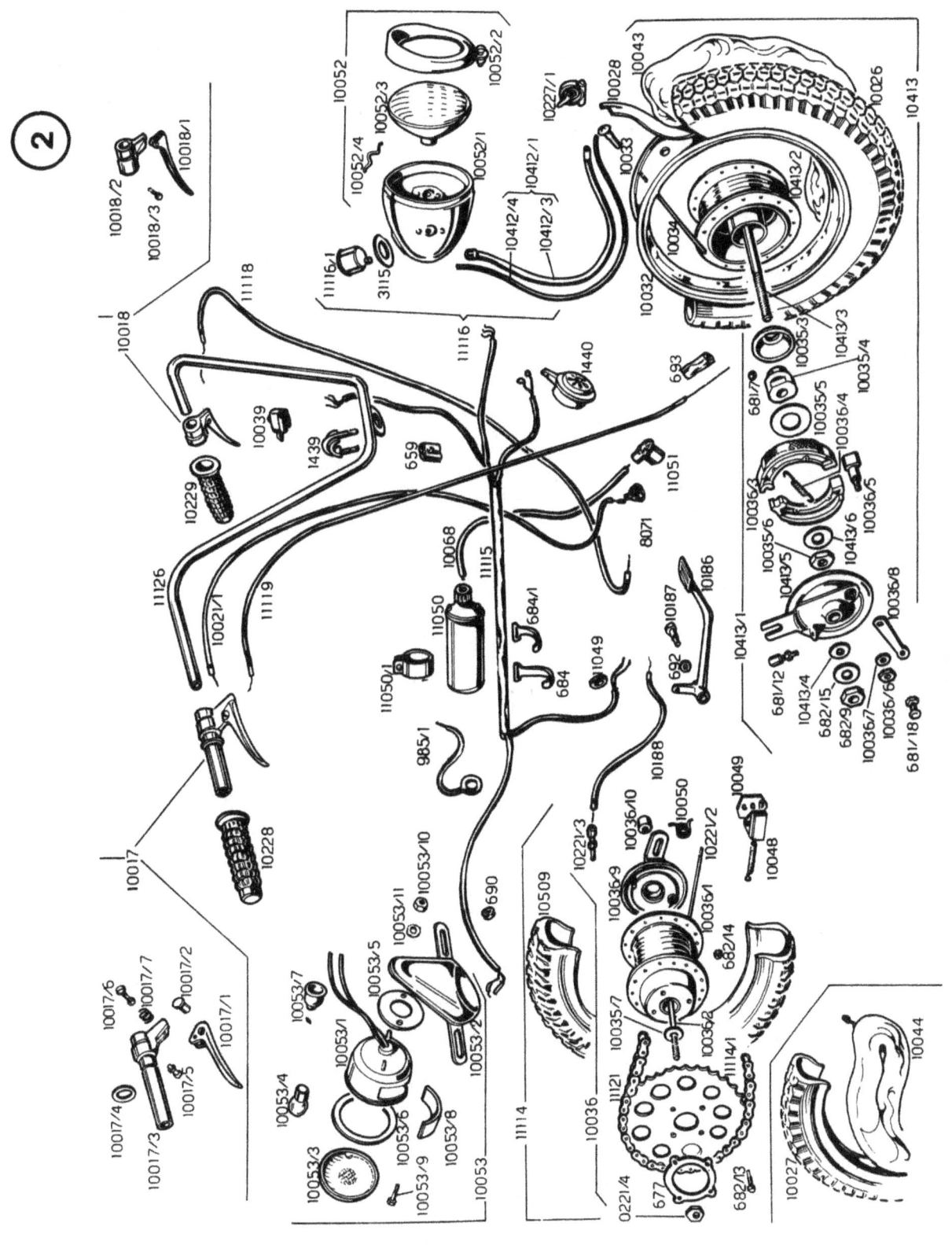

INDIAN-CLYMER MOTORCYCLE DIVISION	GROUP CRANKCASE Refer to: (Photo No. 3 Page No. 12)		Page No 10

Refer. No.	Part number	No. Pcs.	DESCRIPTION
1	20 - 1122	1	Crankcase with bushes
1a	20 - 1123	1	Crankcase with bearings
2	359 - 11 - 121	1	Bush
3	550 - 11 - 212	1	Bush
4	20 - 1130	1	R.H. cover complete
5	6111312189	1	Screw
6	6111312191	2	Screw
7	20 - 1141	1	L.H. cover
8	351 - 11 - 201	1	Plug
9	792	2	Gasket
10	6111462100	1	Screw
11	150 - 11 - 061	1	Gasket
12	05 - 1116	1	Stud
13	6117011084	4	Washer
14	6111352075	6	Screw
15	359 - 11 - 033	1	Seal under L.H. cover
16	611131217	6	Screw
17	6111332104	3	Screw
18	05 - 1105	1	Cylinder barrel gasket
19	359 - 11 - 031	4	Bolt
20	6114012006	4	Nut
21	6117011064	4	Washer
22	555 - 11 - 007	2	Dowel bush
23	6146336004/C3	1	Ball bearing
24	982	2	Gasket
25	359 - 11 - 132	1	Gasket
26	614637636303/C3	2	Ball bearing
27	6146366202/C3	2	Ball bearing
28	6129310035	1	Circlip
29	6111312113	2	Screw
30	6129310042	1	Circlip
31	6111032169	1	Screw

| | INDIAN-CLYMER MOTORCYCLE DIVISION | | GROUP CRANKCASE Refer to: (Photo No. 3 Page No. 12) | Page No 11 |

Refer. No.	Part number	No. Pcs.	DESCRIPTION
32	353 - 11 - 114	1	Gasket
33	05 - 1117	1	Crankcase gasket
34	05 - 1115	1	Cocer
35	793	2	Ring rubber
36	20 - 1137	1	Cower
38	20 - 1133	1	Washer
39	20 - 1132	1	Ring
40	781	1	Gasket
41	977	1	Ring
42	20 - 1136	1	Cower
43	6111552069	3	Screw
44	20 - 1113	2	Dowel bush
45	20 - 1114	1	Dowel bush
46	20 - 1138	1	Gasket
47	11049	1	Grommet

page n.12

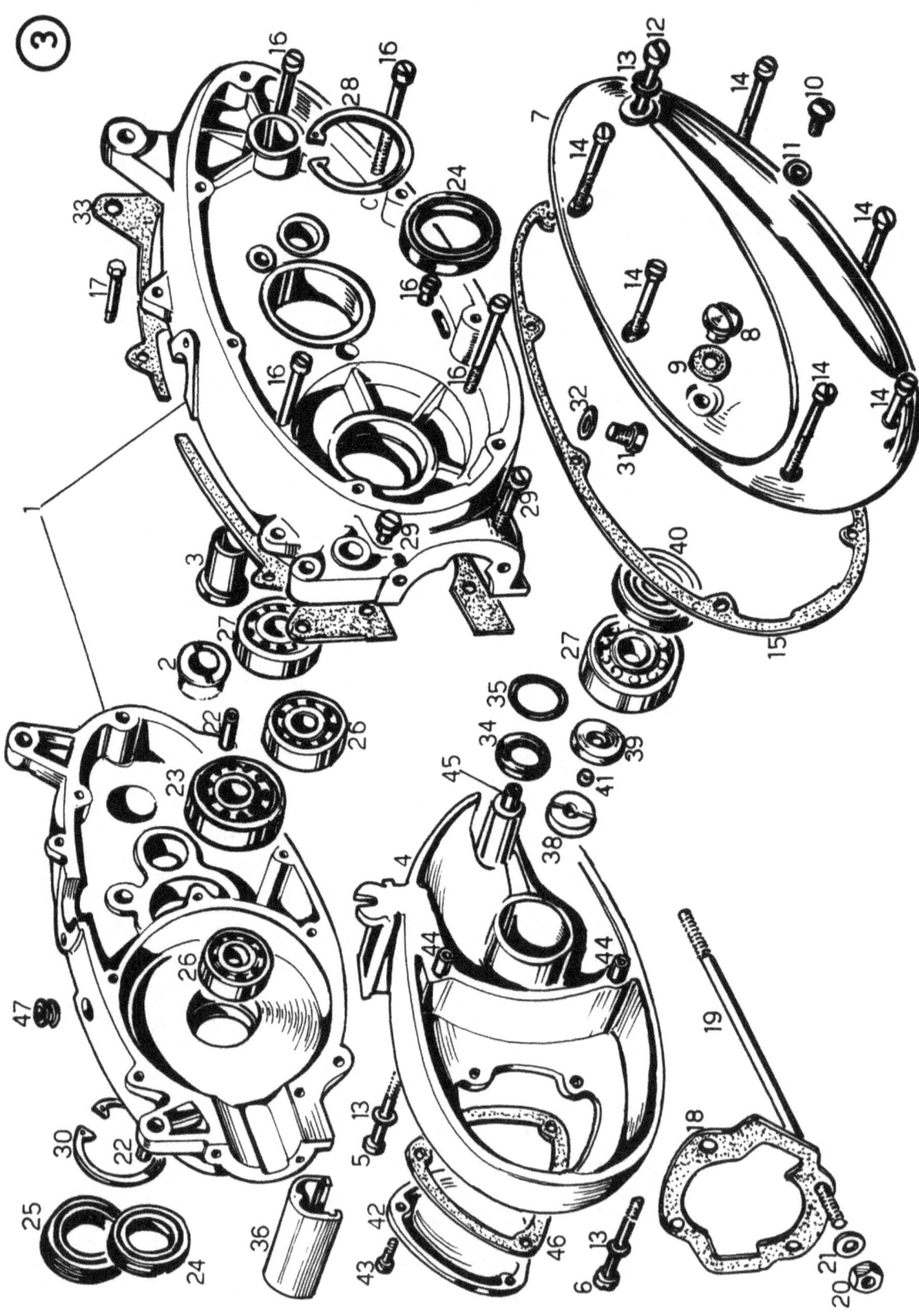

	INDIAN-CLYMER MOTORCYCLE DIVISION		GROUP COMPLETE CONNECTING ROD Refer to: (Photo No. 4 Page No. 15)	Page No 13

Refer. No.	Part number	No. Pcs.	DESCRIPTION
1	20 - 1205	1	Crankshaft and connecting rod
2	20 - 1207	1	R.H. crankshaft
3	20 - 1208	1	L.H. crankshaft
4	20 - 1225	1	Piston
-	20 - 1226		Piston 1st rebore
-	20 - 1227		Piston 2nd rebore
-	20 - 1228		Piston 3rd rebore
-	20 - 1229		Piston 4th rebore
5	359 - 12 - 014	3	Piston ring
-	359 - 12 - 015		Piston ring 1st rebore
-	359 - 12 - 016		Piston ring 2nd rebore
-	359 - 12 - 017		Piston ring 3rd rebore
-	359 - 12 - 018		Piston ring 4th rebore
6	05 - 1221	1	Gudgeon pin
7	05 - 1222	2	Wire circlip
8	05 - 1223	1	Sprocket
9	6117400122	1	Washer
10	6114030112	1	Nut
11	355 - 12 - 033	1	Securing peg
12	05 - 1232	1	Bush
13	05 - 1261	1	Connecting rod with pin and roller

INDIAN-CLYMER MOTORCYCLE DIVISION		GROUP CYLINDER COMPLETE Refer to: (Photo No. 5 Page No. 15)	Page No. 14

Refer. No.	Part number	No. Pcs.	DESCRIPTION
1	20 - 1400	1	Cylinder complete
2	359 - 13 - 013	1	Bush
3	20 - 1404	1	Cylinder head
4	6111781104	2	Fastening screw
5	6111781073	2	Fastening screw
6	14 - 8 - RZ	1	Spark plug

page n. 15

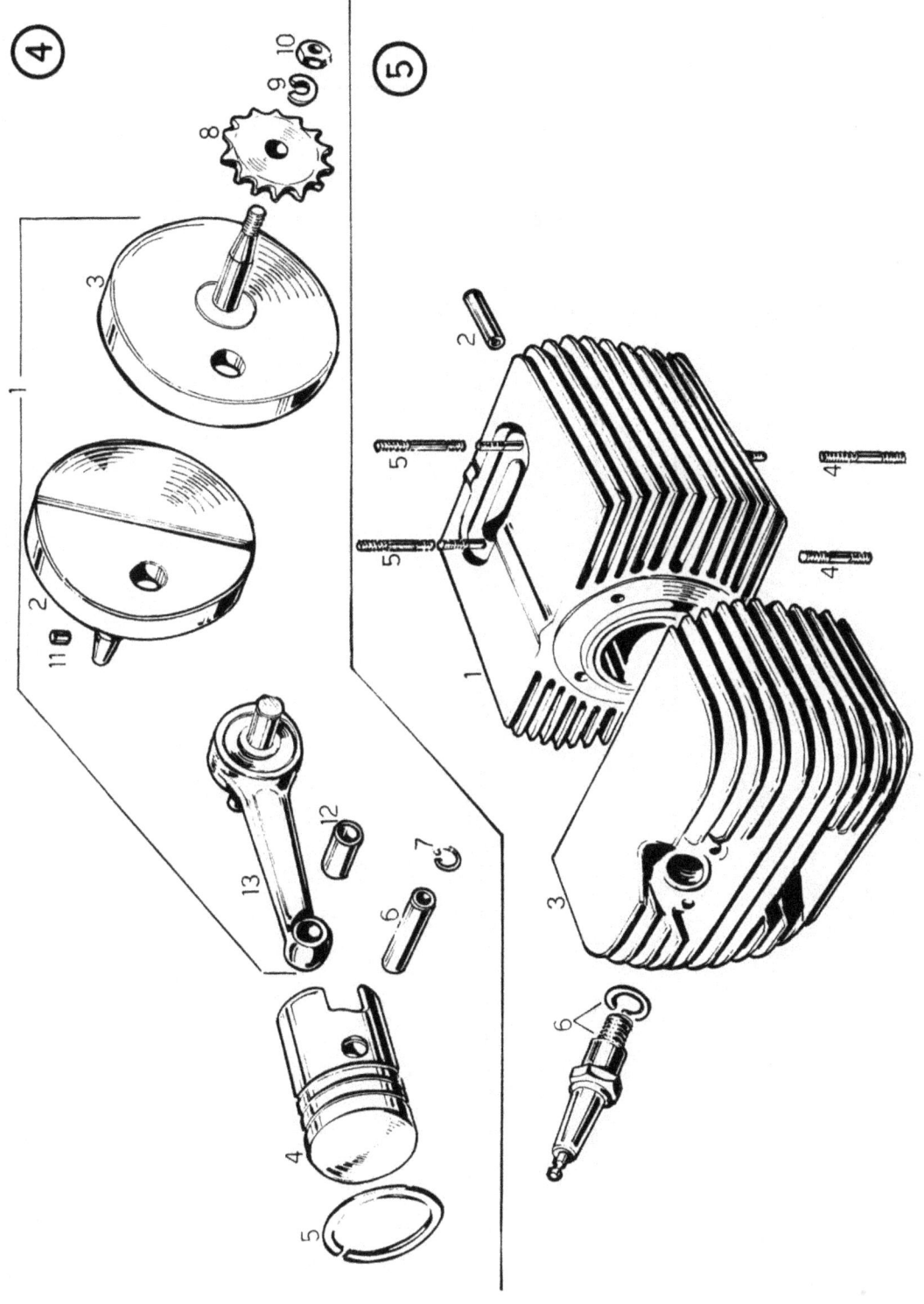

INDIAN-CLYMER MOTORCYCLE DIVISION	GROUP CARBURETTOR PIPE Refer to: (Photo No. 6 Page No. 18)	Page No 16

Refer. No.	Part number	No. Pcs.	DESCRIPTION
19	6111012073	2	Bolt
20	6114012005	4	Nut
21	6117400051	6	Washer
22	20 - 1533	1	Carburettor stub
23	05 - 1506	1	Seal
24	05 - 1541	1	Seal

			GROUP	Page No 17
INDIAN-CLYMER MOTORCYCLE DIVISION			SILENCER	
		Refer to:	(Photo No. 7 Page No. 18)	

Refer. No.	Part number	No. Pcs.	DESCRIPTION
2	6111032103	2	Bolt
3	6114012006	5	Nut
4	6117402061	5	Washer
5	20 - 1615	1	Bolt
6	20 - 1611	1	Silencer body-welded
7	05 - 1612	1	Baffle-welded
8	05 - 1613	1	Tail paper complete
10	05 - 1627	1	Tail paper
11	20 - 1632	1	Ending
12	05 - 1635	1	Lid
13	05 - 1638	1	Seal
14	05 - 1605	1	Seal

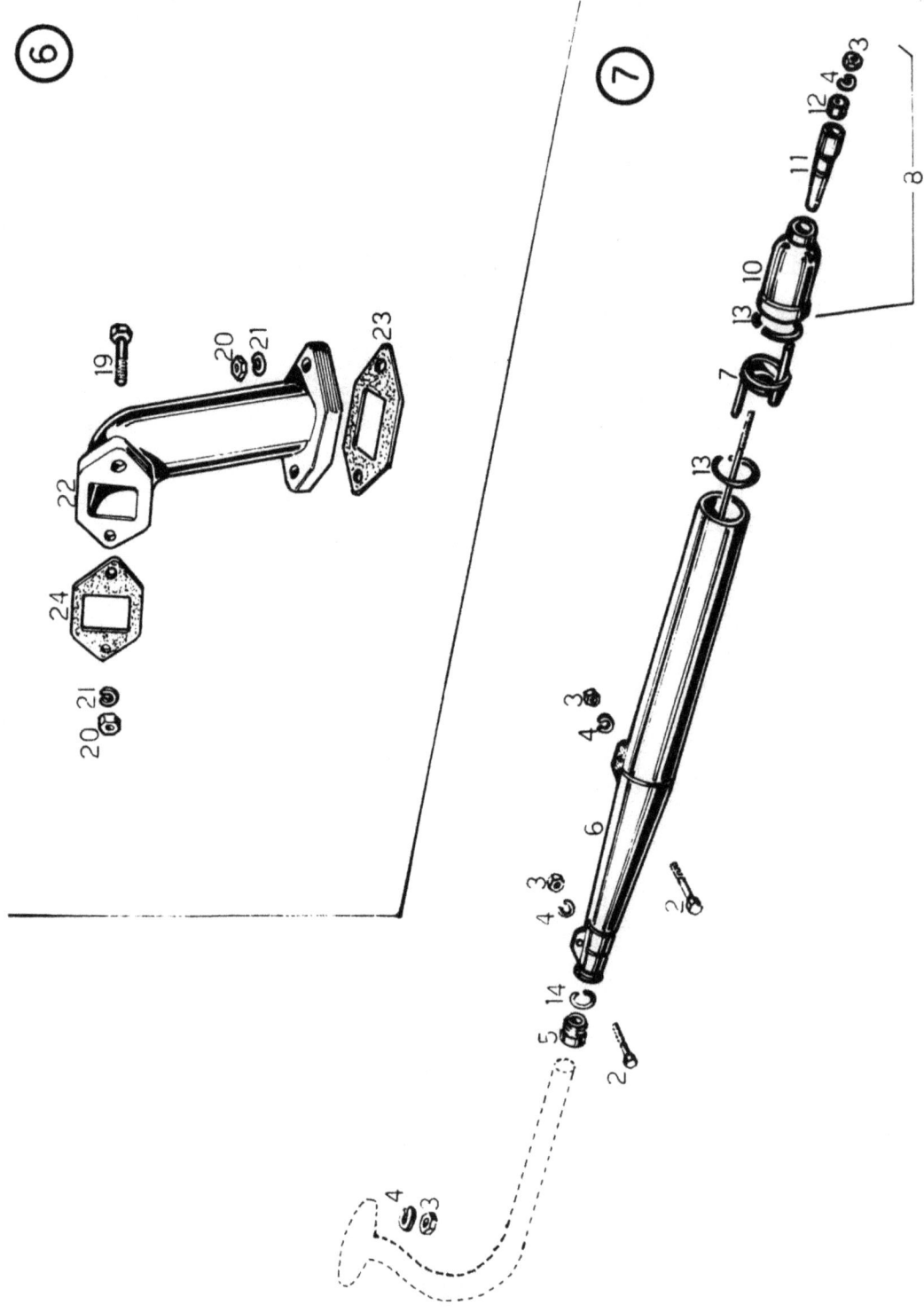

	INDIAN-CLYMER MOTORCYCLE DIVISION	GROUP GEAR-BOX AND KICK STARTER GEARS Refer to: (Photo No. 8 Page No. 20)	Page No. 19

Refer. No.	Part number	No. Pcs.	DESCRIPTION
1	20 - 2220	1	Main shaft
2	20 - 2222	1	Lay shaft
3	20 - 2205	1	1st gear 13T., 24T.
4	20 - 2223	1	2nd gear 20T.
5	20 - 2213	1	Driving gear with hub 23T.
6	359 - 22 - 037	1	Ring
7	550 - 22 - 050	1	Gearbox sprocket 13T.
8	555 - 56 - 302	1	Nut
9	20 - 2232	1	Circlip
10	20 - 2216	1	Speedometer shaft
11	05 - 2227	1	Kick starter ratchet with pin
12	20 - 2229	1	2nd gear 18T.
13	550 - 22 - 046	1	Kick starter spring
14	550 - 22 - 030	1	Kick starter pedal complete
15	359 - 22 - 038	1	Kick starter pedal key
16	6114013006	1	Nut
17	6117012064	1	Washer
20	20 - 2215	1	Ratchet with shaft
21	550 - 22 - 031	1	Kick starter pedal
22	150 - 22 - 050	1	Pedal
23	150 - 22 - 053	1	Pedal rubber
24	150 - 22 - 051	1	Spring
25	150 - 22 - 052	1	Washer
26	151 - 22 - 051	1	Circlip
27	6121500455	1	Peg

page n. 20

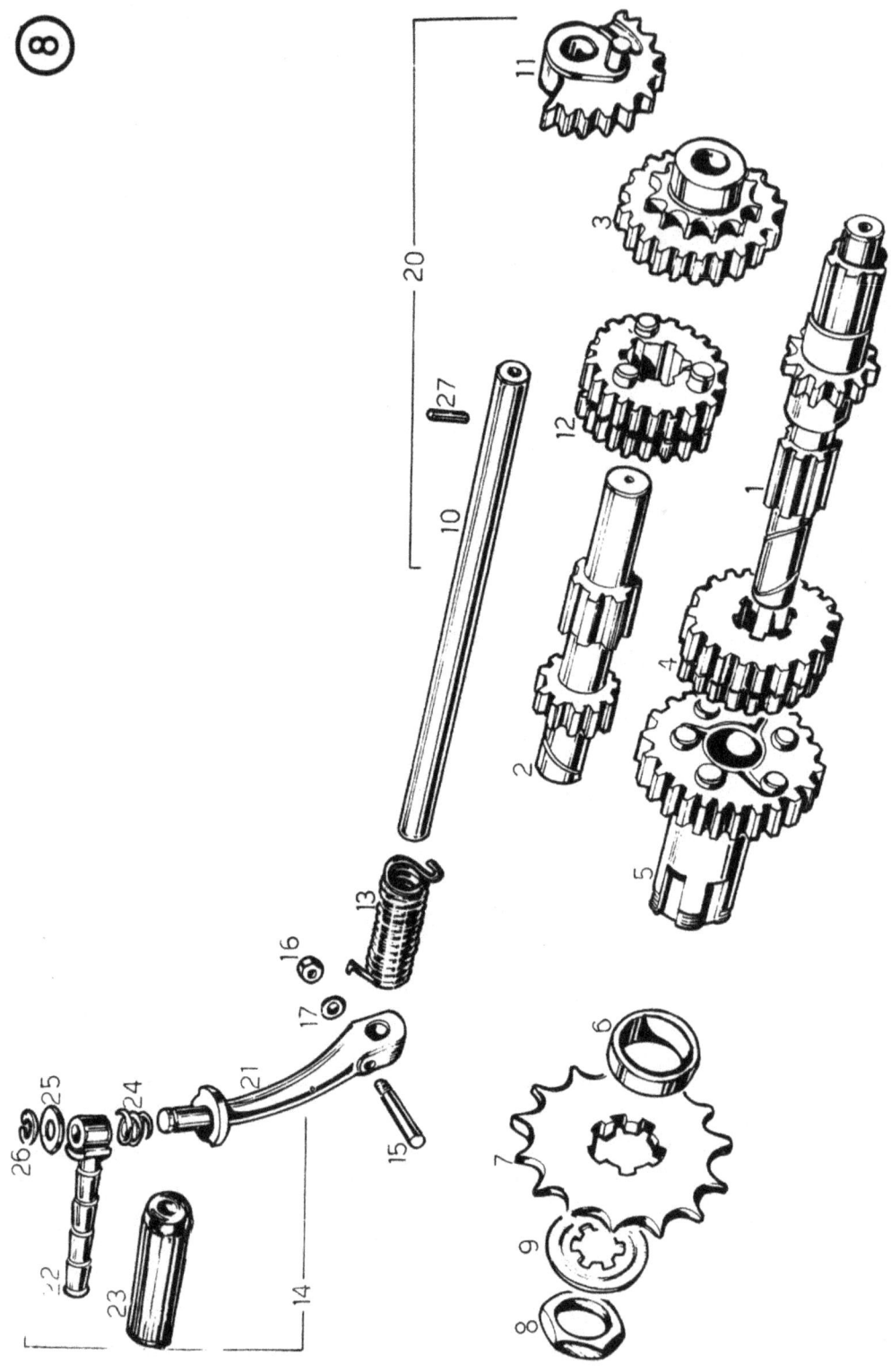

INDIAN-CLYMER MOTORCYCLE DIVISION	GROUP SELECTOR AND GEAR Refer to: (Photo No. 9 Page No. 23)	Page No 21

Refer. No.	Part number	No. Pcs.	DESCRIPTION
1	20 – 2410	1	Foot gear change mechanism
2	555 – 24 – 032	2	Spring
3	359 – 24 – 010	1	Fork complete
4	20 – 2403	1	Guide
6	355 – 24 – 012	1	Pedal rubber
7	05 – 2118	1	Rod
8	550 – 24 – 135	1	Spring
9	550 – 10 – 012	1	Screw
10	6111332104	1	Screw
11	6117402061	1	Washer
12	6129290009	1	Securing ring
13	20 – 2405	1	Gear change pedal welded
14	05 – 2128	1	Pin – welded
15	05 – 2127	1	Insert
16	6114011008	1	Nut
17	6117401082	1	Washer
18	6129290006	1	Circlip
19	6117012084	1	Washer

INDIAN-CLYMER MOTORCYCLE DIVISION	GROUP CLUTCH Refer to: (Photo No. 10 Page No. 23)	Page No. 22

Refer. No.	Part number	No. Pcs.	DESCRIPTION
1	05 - 2101	2	Clutch chainwheel complete
2	05 - 2104	1	Fixed plate complete
3	05 - 2108	1	Pressure plate complete
4	05 - 2111	1	Plate
5	05 - 2112	5	Spring
6	05 - 2113	5	Cup
7	359 - 28 - 043	5	Washer
8	6129290004	6	Securing ring
9	05 - 2116	1	Circlip
10	05 - 2114	1	Nut
11	05 - 2115	1	Clutch operating rod
12	359 - 28 - 013	32	Cork insert
13	828	1	Primary chain 3/8x3/8 in. 44 links
14	6136800005	3	Ball
15	20 - 2125	1	Clutch operating rod
16	20 - 2121	1	Operating lever
17	20 - 2124	1	Lever pin
18	20 - 2123	1	Grub screw
19	6114032006	2	Nut

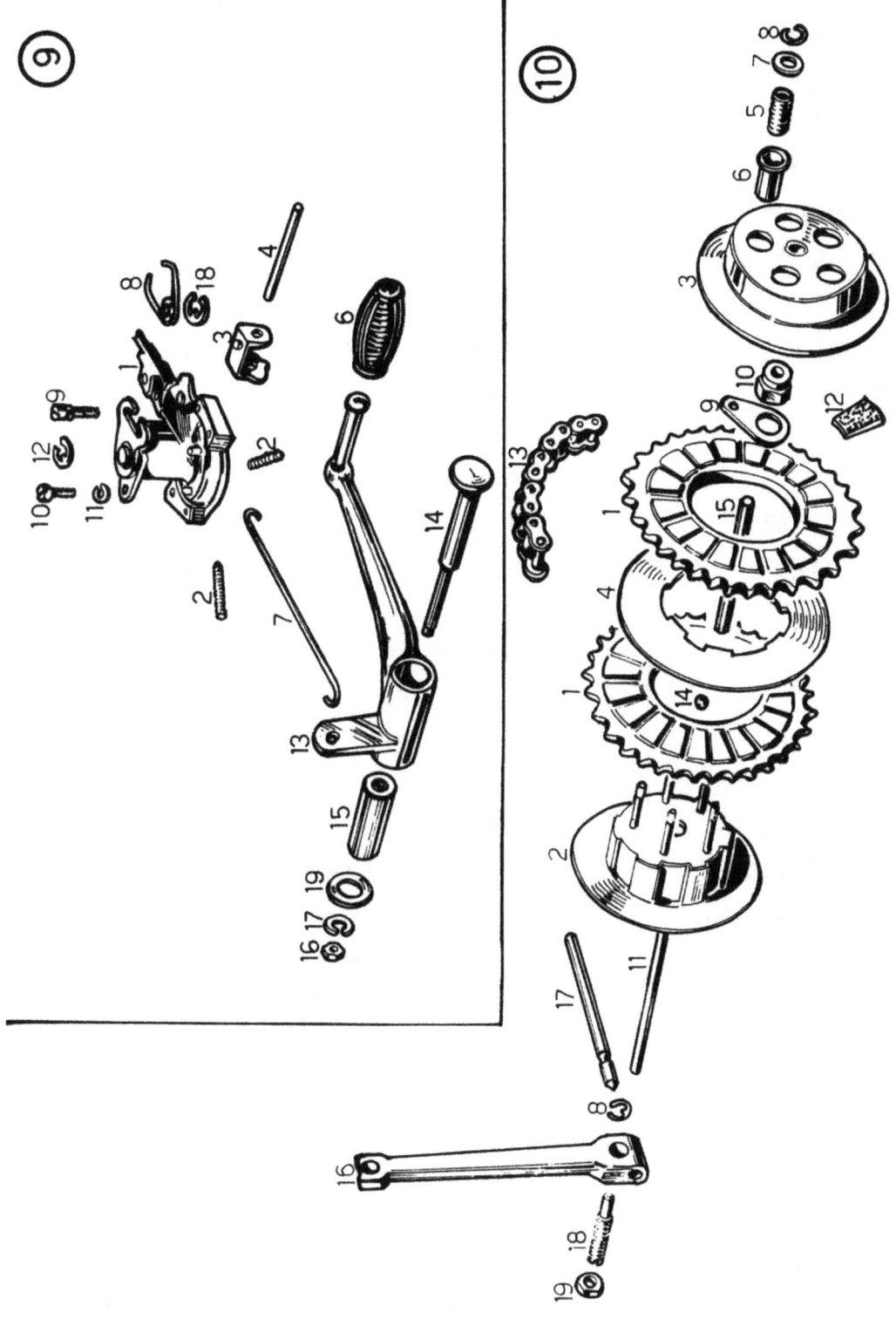

| | INDIAN-CLYMER MOTORCYCLE DIVISION | GROUP FLYWHEEL Refer to: (Photo No. 11 Page No. 25) | Page No 24 |

Refer. No.	Part number	No. Pcs.	DESCRIPTION
1	05 - 6120	1	Magneto complete
2	05 - 6128	1	Stator body with wiper
3	05 - 6127	1	Condenser bracket
4	6123010287	1	Rivet
5	05 - 6132	1	Illuminative pole complete
6	05 - 6154	1	Ignition pole complete
7	05 - 6143	1	Numeral pole complete
8	05 - 6170	1	Dynamo rotor
9	05 - 6125	1	Cam
10	6111052083	1	Screw
11	6111312042	2	Screw
12	6111312048	4	Screw
13	6117402051	3	Washer
14	05 - 6105	1	Condenser
15	6111312076	2	Screw
16	359 - 61 - 012	2	Rest
17	355 - 61 - 230	1	Felt
18	6123011205	1	Rivet
19	355 - 61 - 240	1	Contact holder complete
20	355 - 61 - 260	1	Contact breaker arm
21	355 - 61 - 211	2	Insulation washer
22	6117332041	1	Washer
23	355 - 61 - 212	1	Insulation washer
24	6111032040	1	Screw
25	6111312039	1	Screw
26	6114012004	1	Nut
27	6117402043	7	Washer
28	355 - 61 - 214	1	Washer
29	05 - 6124	1	Connector

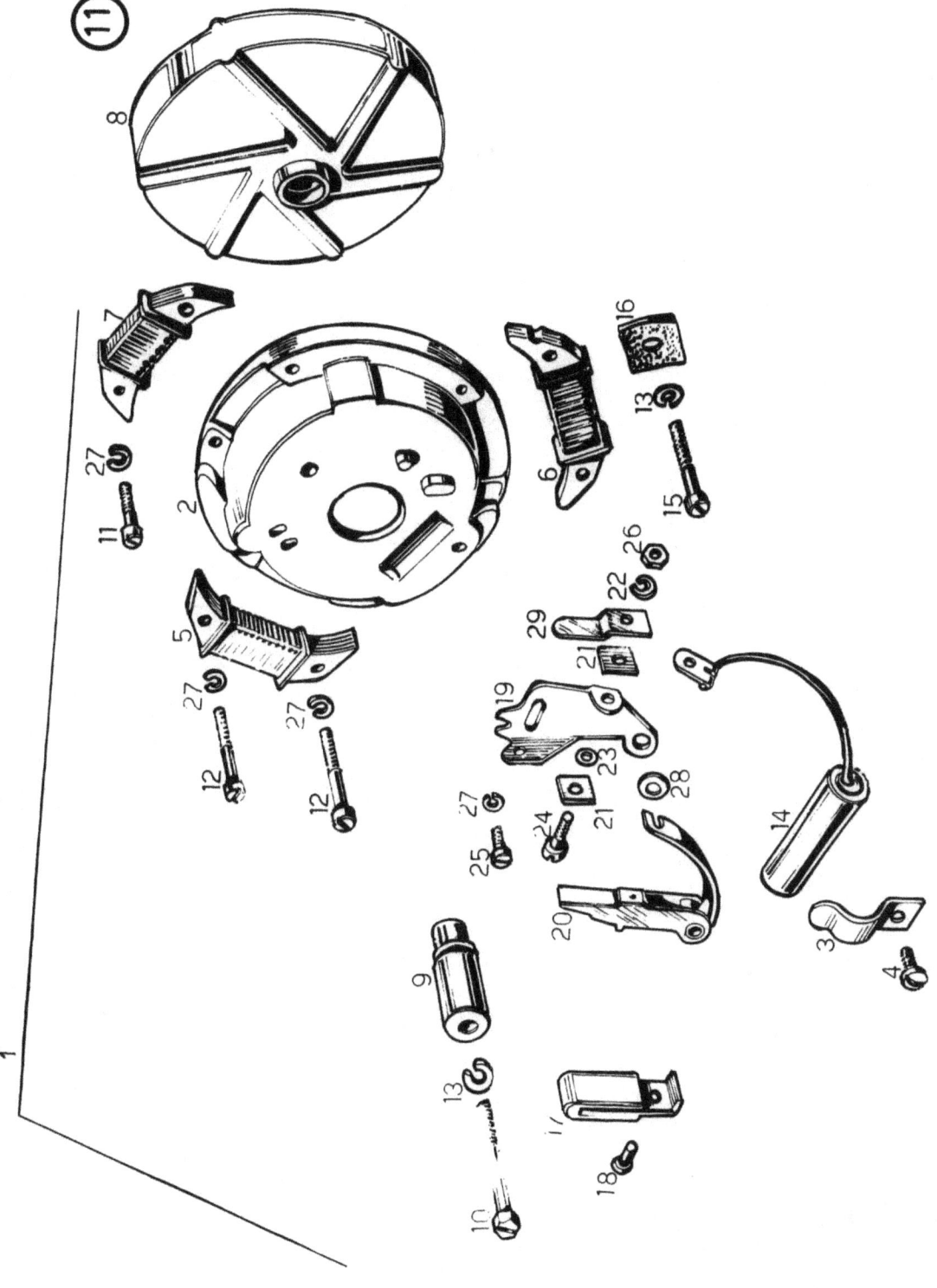

	INDIAN-CLYMER MOTORCYCLE DIVISION	GROUP JAWA CARBURETTOR Refer to: (Photo No. 12 Page No. 27)	Page No 26

Refer. No.	Part number	No. Pcs.	DESCRIPTION
1	11 - 2739	1	Carburettor
2	937 - 0113	1	Carburettor body
3	946 - 0118	1	Float complete
4	937 - 1107	1	Float chamber top
5	107 - 1401	1	Idling jet
8	103 - 3601 - 4	1	Cable guide
9	130 - 0114 - 4	1	Nut
10	706 - 0902	1	Mixing chamber top
11	134 - 0271 - 4	1	Throttle valve spring
12	209 - 0607	1	Throttle valve needle
13	601 - 3701	1	Needle circlip
14	737 - 0434	1	Throttle valve
15	107 - 1501	1	Main jet
16	101 - 2301 - 4	1	Throttle valve adjusting screw
17	134 - 0123 - 4	1	Spring
18	101 - 0801 - 4	2	Top screw
25	201 - 0230	1	Axle
26	604 - 5501	1	Suspension
27	934 - 0113	1	Valve
28	625 - 0248	1	Seal
29	934 - 3504 -	1	Bolt
30	625 - 0121	1	Seal

page n. 27

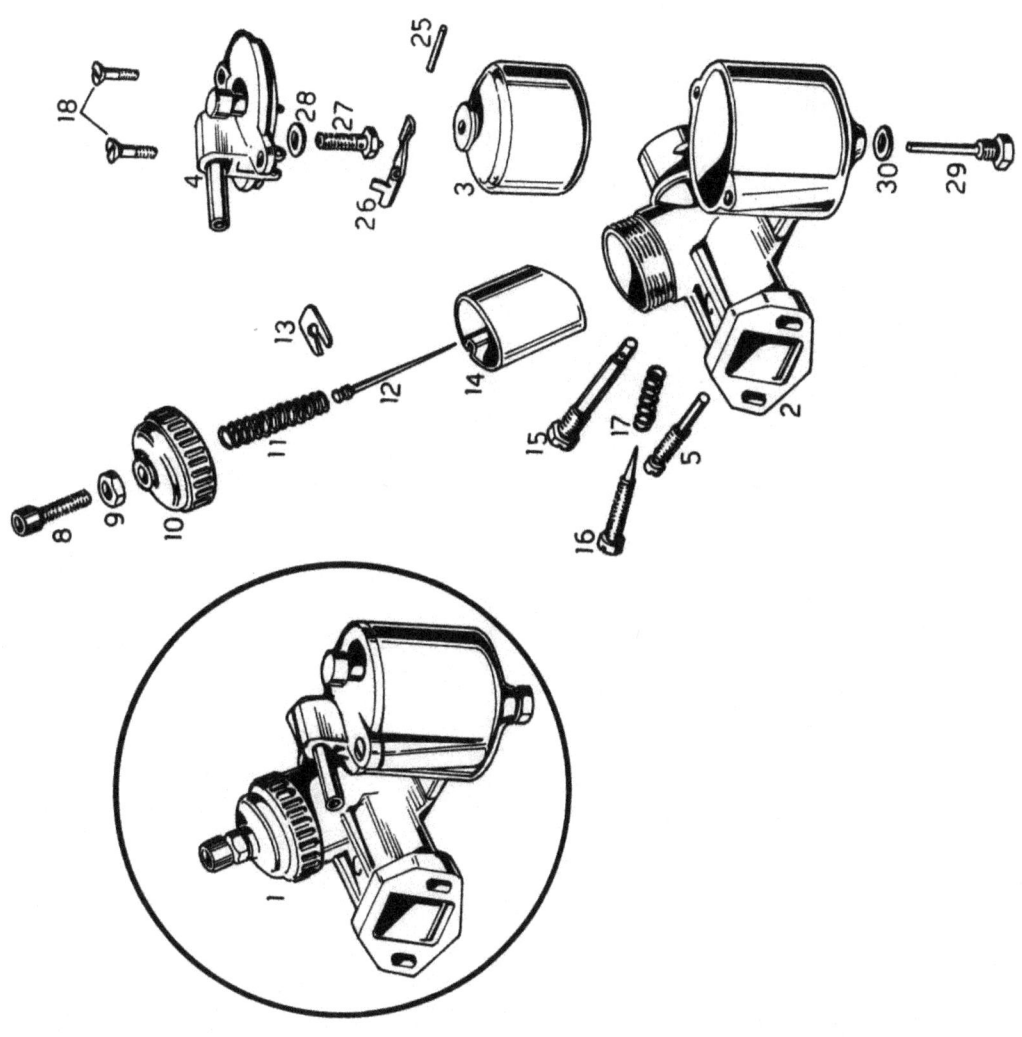

NOTES

BOY RACER

Sales Literature Scrap Book
Pages 43 to 49

Illustrated Parts List
Pages 51 to 73

Indian BOY RACER

A SCALED DOWN ULTRA-LIGHTWEIGHT FOR THE BUDDING ENTHUSIAST IN YOUR FAMILY

SCALED DOWN competition model weighs only 99 pounds. Duplex frame is used, giving extra rigidity.

THE OLD saying, "Good things come in small packages," certainly applies to this scaled down newcomer from Floyd Clymer Motorcycle Division. Carrying the Indian nameplate, this mini-motorcycle is designed for the very young enthusiast ("6 to 16", states the manufacturer) who wishes to try his hand in most types of off-road competition.

Powerplant of this "Boy's Racer" is a 50cc 2-stroke Jawa-CZ engine, with integral 3-speed gearbox. Top speed is claimed to be 50 mph.

To give you an idea of the diminutive size of this model, the wheelbase is 40 inches, saddle height at 23 inches, with tire sizes being 2.125 x 20.

Finished in blue and white, this little Indian has brakes fore and aft with telescopic front forks and swinging arm rear suspension. Price, f.o.b. Los Angeles, is $325.

Young man, the line forms over there to the right.

FINISHED in blue and white, this mini-motorcycle features a 40-inch wheelbase, 23-inch saddle height, two brakes, front and rear suspension.

VETERAN motorcyclist Floyd Clymer poses with newest pride and joy - actually one of many new models he has introduced.

POWERPLANT for little Indian is 50cc 2-stroke Jawa-CZ engine, with 3-speed gearbox built in unit. Top speed of 50 mph is claimed by manufacturer.

FEBRUARY, 1969

Reprinted from the Motor CYCLIST

Gordon Jennings, Editor Cycle Magazine, technical writer and racer, shown here with his wife, Bunnie, and sons, Gordon Jennings III and David. Gordon III is the owner of an Indian Boy Racer. He looks happy, as does young David on the Indian Mini-Mini.

New Indian Boy Racer appeals to youngsters, even Miss Cheryl Parker

Youngsters drool over NEW Indian Boy Racer

INDIAN BOY RACER

Reprinted from Modern Cycle

Out in the desert and around campsites these days one of the more common sights is a group of youngsters putting around on mini-bikes. The speed with which the entire family has taken to motorcycling is hard to believe. A couple of years ago Dad went to the races and Mom and the kids spent the day in and around the pick up. Soon Mom had her own trail bike and the kids were left to fend for themselves along with the other "pit rats." Finally the day arrived when Dad's racer and Mom's trail bike were joined in the back of the truck, by a couple of mini-bikes. At last everybody was happy . . . for a while, at least. Any parent can tell you how fast kids grow and it doesn't take a child too long before he's a size where a mini-bike is too small and a trail bike is too large. When the boy or girl reaches this stage in growth it's usually back to the old pick up. Now there is a machine available that will bring the smiles back to the faces of the kiddies. It's called the Indian Boy Racer and it's the brainchild of Floyd Clymer.

When photographed standing alone the Boy Racer looks very much like something you'd expect to find in the pits at Ascot Park. The moment an adult steps into the picture the little Indian shows its true scale. Standing 23 inches at the saddle the Boy Racer fills the gap between the mini-bike and the full sized motorcycle.

Power for the Boy Racer is supplied by a 50cc engine made by the Jawa-CZ firm. This unit construction mill features a three speed gearbox and is capable of moving the machine along at speeds close to fifty miles per hour. An Italian Dellorto carburetor feeds the gas/oil mixture to the combustion chamber and induction is controlled by the rise and fall of the piston. We found the Boy Racer to be a cold blooded little devil and use of the choke was necessary in almost all instances. Fortunately the choke is extremely easy to operate; it's set with a lever on the body of the carburetor and turned off by rolling the throttle past the 2/3's point.

The kick starter lever is on the right side of the machine and moves forward to bring the machine to life. This kick starter was one of the new items on the bike we could find fault with. Movement was limited by the footpeg and brake pedal and the need to kick forward was just plain awkward. Gear changes are made from the left side of the bike with the pattern: up for low then down for the remaining two speeds. Because of the complex linkage in the shifting mechanism gear changes are a bit on the sloppy side, but a positive move of the toe will get you the desired cog.

No great amount of pressure is necessary to move the clutch lever, however, the lever is one of the few things on the machine that isn't scaled down to size. A couple of our staff member's children had trouble moving the lever until we backed off on the cable adjuster and installed a spacer between the lever blade and its mount. Once this was done the blade was closer to the handgrip and the kids had no further problems.

It's very easy to fall into the trap of considering a 50cc machine an underpowered bike. Frequently this is true, but in the case of the Boy Racer the 50cc engine delivers plenty of umph. Most of the performance can be credited to the power to weight ratio. Full of gas and ready to run the Indian weighs just over 100 pounds. Add a rider who weighs the same (or less) and you can see what we mean by a good power to weight ratio. The Boy Racer was designed to meet the demands of a certain sized rider; with a rider of the intended size aboard the bike performs quite well.

For a machine that many adults would consider a toy the Boy Racer is remarkably sophisticated; the frame is a case in point. Here again we find a device that looks like its been scaled down from a much larger motorcycle. A single backbone tube connects the steering head to the front of the sub-frame structure and double down tubes cradle the engine. Diagonal tubes connecting the cradle tubes to the tops of the rear shocks provide the triangulation for the sub-frame. The swinging arm is fabricated of tubular stock and axle adjustment is made by means of cam-type washers. The tubing used in the construction of the Boy Racer is of a size you'd expect to find on a full sized motorcycle and the welding is top quality.

Even one of our two hundred pound test riders couldn't detect any signs of frame flex. He did look a little odd though, considering his size and the size of the machine! As a matter of fact the Boy Racer is difficult for an adult to ride. It's meant for a youngster and a full grown man has trouble bending himself to reach the shift lever and brake pedal.

Another thing we liked about the concept behind the little Indian was the use of big wheels. Both spoked wheels are 20 inches in diameter and both carry 2.125x20 tires that look like those commonly found on bicycles. Because of the size of the wheels, and the machine in general, a youngster can become familiar with the characteristics he'll encounter when he moves up to a regular motorcycle. Broadsliding is an example: try to get sideways on a mini-bike and you'll find yourself on your gourd. The little wheels just don't take to sliding. On the other hand the Boy Racer will broadslide very nicely.

Both wheels are laced to full width finned alloy hubs and the hubs contain a braking system that would be acceptable to a moto-cross racer. On a machine the size of the Boy Racer brakes of this sort are just so much icing on the cake. Both brakes are cable operated and, needless to say, both do an excellent job of stopping the bike.

Considering the disparity in size among youngsters between six and twelve it's amazing that the Boy Racer fits so many kids so well. As delivered the little Indian is set up for use on smooth dirt. (The fact that it carries no lights or other street equipment makes it illegal for use on the pavement). With some minor modifications, a knobby tire and a skid plate for the engine, the machine could be made capable of going just about anywhere.

The Indian Boy Racer makes a very good first impression. The little bike offers a jewel-like appearance. The quality of finish is of a very high order. The paint is well applied and the metallic blue and white gastank is nicely shaped. Plastic is used in the construction of the number plates and front fender and the entire seat/fender assembly is covered in an easily cleaned upholstery material.

Price for the Indian Boy Racer is $325.00 F.O.B. Los Angeles. We think that the Boy Racer offers features found on no other machine designed for the younger members of the family.

Famous Personalities Who Own Indians are Andretti and Granatelli.

MARIO ANDRETTI, 500-Mile winner, and his young son on Indian Boy Racer. Publicist Bill Marvel of Sports Headliners (in center), and Clymer on left.

Andretti's son, Rick, is thrilled by Indian Boy Racer. He sat on it for an hour.

STP President, winning race car owner, the world famous GRANATELLI with Mario's son. Andy was an Indian Scout owner as a youngster and now owns an Indian Papoose.

While travel is limited the action of the front forks is good. A fine set of brakes are housed in full width alloy hubs. Front fender is flexible plastic which should resist prangs.

The seat resembles the units usually found on road racers. Padding is sufficient for the younger members of the family. Long seat base extends to the rear to act as a fender.

50cc three speed engine is a product of the Jawa-CZ firm. The Italian Dellorto carburetor incorporates a choke that snaps to the off position when the throttle is rolled full on.

Indian BOY RACER

A SCALED DOWN ULTRA-LIGHTWEIGHT FOR THE BUDDING ENTHUSIAST IN YOUR FAMILY

THE OLD saying, "Good things come in small packages," certainly applies to this scaled down newcomer from Floyd Clymer Motorcycle Division. Carrying the Indian nameplate, this mini-motorcycle is designed for the very young enthusiast ("6 to 16", states the manufacturer) who wishes to try his hand in most types of off-road competition.

Powerplant of this "Boy's Racer" is a 50cc 2-stroke Jawa-CZ engine, with integral 3-speed gearbox. Top speed is claimed to be 50 mph.

To give you an idea of the diminutive size of this model, the wheelbase is 40 inches, saddle height at 23 inches, with tire sizes being 2.125 x 20.

Finished in blue and white, this little Indian has brakes fore and aft with telescopic front forks and swinging arm rear suspension. Price, f.o.b. Los Angeles, is $325.

Young man, the line forms over there to the right.

THE INDIAN BOY RACER

IT'S NOT A MINI-BIKE IT'S A MINI-MOTORCYCLE.

FLOYD CLYMER MOTORCYCLE DIVISION

222 N. Virgil Avenue • Los Angeles, California 90004
Phone: (213) 388-5119 • Cable: "Clymer" Los Angeles

MANUFACTURERS
Indian Motorcycles made in Italy
•
U.S. and Canadian distributors for
Clymer-Minarelli
cycle and minibike 2-stroke engines
and
Clymer-Tartarini Telescopic Forks
and
Royal-Enfield British Motorcycles
for all states west of Mississippi River

IMPORTANT NOTICE

SPECIAL OFFER!

These INDIANS are stylish, well designed and engineered, and beautifully finished with excellent paint jobs. They are actually small motorcycles or super (large) minibikes, yet small enough to fit easily into a station wagon, passenger car trunk (if handlebars are lowered), camper, truck, airplane, boat or mobile home.

Easier to ride and SAFER - They are easier riding and SAFER than most minibikes because they have speeds up to 50 mph, with a 2-stroke 50cc engine that performs more like a 90cc than a 50. Two brakes, front and rear, and full spring suspension make for E-Z riding and handling as they have wire spoke wheels and Pirelli tires (10 x 3.00 front, 10 x 3.50 rear - larger than most minibikes).

INDIAN, the oldest name in U. S. motorcycling, offers the following features, many of them exclusive, on these models:

PAPOOSE -- 4-speed, 50 mph, the best of our minis! Price is $345.00 F.O.B. Los Angeles, crated ready to ship, with regular road tires. Dual seat. Add $10.00 per wheel if you want knobby (trail) tires. Specify red or blue color.

PONYBIKE -- 3-speed, 50 mph, trail bike special. Price $295.00 crated ready to ship, with road tires and dual seat. Add $10.00 per wheel for knobby (trail) tires. Specify gold or red color.

Lights, front and rear, and speedometer included as standard equipment on Papoose and Ponybike models.

BOY RACER -- With 2.25 x 16" tires and wire spoke wheels. 50 mph. For kids 6 to 18 years of age. It's really too small for adults, as it is a real scaled down motorcycle, but not a toy. It's a practical bike. The larger-than-scooter wheels enables the rider to "broadside" on dirt corners just like a big bike. Specify red or blue color. $325.00. Add $10.00 per wheel if you want knobby (trail) tires. Has no lights or speedo, as it is strictly an off-the-road model.

INFORMATION ON ABOVE BIKES --

PRICES -- are F.O.B. our Los Angeles warehouse. Includes delivery to airport or freight office (either motor truck or rail).

World's Largest Publisher of Books on Autos, Motorcycles, Racing and Americana

SHIPPED COMPLETE -- Not in knocked down kit form. Packed one to a crate.
Easy to set up. Only necessary to uncrate, attach handlebars and footpegs
(about 20 minutes work), add mixture of regular gas and oil and you are
ready to roll.

TERMS -- Cash. We have no time payment plan; however, buyer may deduct 3%
cash discount if remittance is sent with order. If machines are sent C.O.D.
or sight draft through a bank, the 3% discount does not apply - only if remittance is sent with order.

SPARE PARTS -- We have large stocks in Los Angeles. Almost overnight service
to any U. S. location.

GUARANTEE -- 30 days or 1,000 miles, whichever comes first.

APPROXIMATE SHIPPING COSTS -- Machines weigh 99 to 106 lbs. Crated about
115 lbs. Motor truck is cheapest and charges run from $4.00 to $6.00 per
machine to West Coast states (3 to 4 days arrival time); $12.00 to $14.00
to Mountain states (5 to 7 days arrival time); $15.00 to $16.00 to Midwest
states (8 to 10 days arrival time); $18.00 to $20.00 to Eastern states and
far South (12 to 14 days arrival time). You pay transportation upon arrival.

AIR SHIPMENTS - You may want air shipment, and air freight is very reasonable. Add about 50% of above estimates for air freight. Usually overnight
delivery to large cities with airports suitable for jets. Another day or so
if transfer is necessary for air or truck freight to small towns or cities
with small airports. If you are near a large city, it is best and faster if
we send directly to the airport, marked "HOLD FOR PICKUP" (example: Notify
John Doe - phone POdunk 666-8888).

For instance, we shipped a Papoose to a Pontiac dealer, marked "hold for
pickup at TWA office Pittsburgh, Pa." He drove 70 miles and had his bike
at 9:00 A.M. the following morning. It would have taken two or three more
days had it been transferred to a truck to haul 70 miles to his small town.

TITLE AND INSTRUCTIONS -- We send these by air mail when the bike is shipped.
The "Certificate of Origin" is your bill of sale, and we include a paid
invoice and instructions for setting up and operation.

Indian TECHNICAL DATA CHART

	PONYBIKE	BOY RACER	PAPOOSE
Engine:	Jawa M-20	Jawa M-20	Minarelli P4 "Sport"
Type:	Two-Stroke	Two-Stroke	Two-Stroke
No. of Cylinders:	One	One	One
Displacement:	50cc.	50cc.	50cc.
Bore:	38mm.	38mm.	38mm.
Stroke:	44mm.	44mm.	42mm.
Horsepower:	4.8	4.8	4.8
Compression Ratio:	8.0:1	8.0:1	8.0:1
Carburetor:	Jikov	Dellorto SHA 14.14	Dellorto UA125
Fuel Capacity:	1.2 Gal.	1.2 Gal.	1.2 Gal.
Lubrication:	Gas/Oil Mixture	Gas/Oil Mixture	Gas/Oil Mixture
Clutch:	Multi. Disc in Oil	Multi. Disc in Oil	Multi. Disc in Oil
Primary Drive:	Chain	Chain	Helical Gear
Ignition & Lights:	Magneto, 6V-20W	Magneto, 6V. - 20W.	Magneto, 6V - 20W.
Gear Ratios: 1st	28.99:1	28.99:1	15.22:1
2nd	15.21:1	15.21:1	9.25:1
3rd	10.28:1	10.28:1	6.64:1
4th	-	-	5.10:1
Final Drive Ratio:	3.92:1	4.61:1	3.71:1
Tires: (Pirelli)	front-2.25 x 16	front - 2¼ x 16	front - 1.50 x 19
	rear - 2.50 x 16	rear - 2¼ x 16	rear - 1.50 x 19
Suspension: front:	Telescopic Fork	Telescopic Fork	Telescopic Fork
rear:	Swing Arm w/Damper	Swing Arm w/Damper	Swing Arm w/Damper
Weight: (Dry)	106 lbs.	99 lbs.	135 lbs.
Wheelbase:	41 in.	41 in.	38 in.
Ground Clearance:	8 in.	8 in.	8 in.
Foot Peg Height:	9 in.	9.5 in.	9 in.
Seat Height:	25 in.	25 in.	27 in.
Top Speed:	45 m.p.h.	50 m.p.h.	50 m.p.h.
Colors Availible:	Red, Metallic Gold	Red & White, Blue & White	Metallic Red, Metallic Blue

NOTES

| INDIAN-CLYMER MOTORCYCLE DIVISION | GROUP FRAME Refer to: (Photo No. 13 Page No. 30) | Page No 28 |

Part number	No. Pcs.	DESCRIPTION
12300	1	Frame
12301	1	Side stand
618	1	Stand spring
8043	1	Screw
12302	1	Rear fork
2105	2	Bush
1412	1	Pivot TE 12MBx195
12304	1	Front fork complete
12304/1	1	Spider
12304/2	1	R.H. fork leg
12304/3	1	L.H. fork leg
12304/4	1	Plate
695/10	2	Rubber
12304/5	2	Spring
695/14	2	Rubber
12304/6	2	Pin
695/15	2	Screw TE 8x45
695/12	6	Washer ⌀ 8
12304/7	2	Inner tube
695/16	2	Nut 8MA
12304/8	2	Screw TE 8MAx15
12304/9	1	R.H. shadder
12304/10	1	L.H. shadder
12304/11	2	Dust cover
12304/12	2	Ring
12304/13	2	Springs
12305	1	Front fender
12306	1	Rear fender-seat complete
12308	3	Number plate
12310	2	Rear shock absorber mm. 190
608	1	Outer upper steering column bearing
609	1	Outer lower steering column bearing

INDIAN-CLYMER MOTORCYCLE DIVISION	GROUP FRAME Refer to: (Photo No. 13 Page No. 30)	Page No 29

Part number	No. Pcs.	DESCRIPTION
610	1	Inner upper steering column bearing
611	1	Inner lower steering column bearing
613	1	Nut
613/1	2	Washer
612	52	Ball 5/32
12311	1	Chain guard
12312	2	Engine bracket
12313	1	Stones guard
3020	2	Front foot rest
8033	2	Foot rest rubber
848	1	Couple chain stretcher
10046	1	Engine
10046/1	1	Kick starter lever
11122/2	1	Gear change lever
12314	1	Pipe connection engine-carburettor
10057	1	Connection pipe-carburettor
10045	1	Carburettor SHA 14/14 complete
12309	1	Fuel tank
10042	1	Fuel tank plug
652	1	Fuel cock one way
633	1	Fuel cock two ways
634	5	Fuel cock gasket
12316	1	Fuel connection between cocks
12317	1	Fuel connection cock-carburettor
11210	1	Couple "INDIAN" decalco gold
12226	2	Decalco "designed by Tartarini"
12329	1	"BOY RACER" decalco
12318	1	Complete exhaust pipe with muffler
10066	2	Exhaust pipe gasket
10255	1	Muffler cover
12314/1	1	Gasket
12314/2	1	Gasket

page n. 30

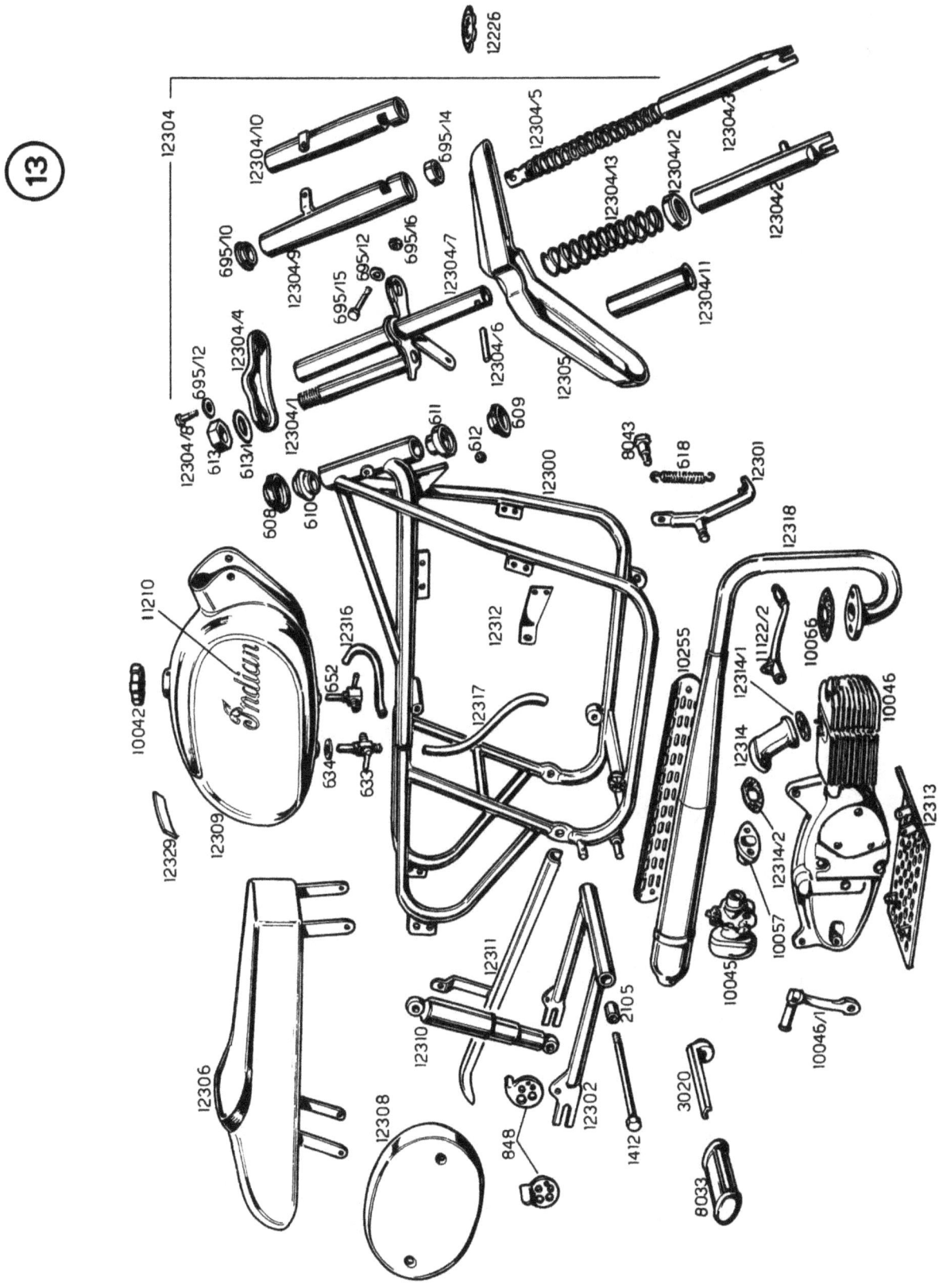

INDIAN-CLYMER MOTORCYCLE DIVISION	GROUP CONTROLS AND WHEELS Refer to: (Photo No. 14 Page No. 34)	Page No 31

Part number	No. Pcs.	DESCRIPTION
12320	1	Complete handle bar
12320/1	1	Naked handle bar
12320/2	1	Front brake R.H. lever
12320/3	1	Clutch L.H. lever
12320/4	2	Screw
12320/5	2	Tender
1319	1	Gas control
1439	2	Little fork
12321	1	L.H. handle
12322	1	R.H. handle
659	2	Hold-fast
12333	1	Wire gas control
12334	1	Wire clutch control
12335	1	Wire front brake control
10219	1	Wire rear brake control
12323	2	Tire 2-1/4 - 16 regular
12324	2	Tube 6A 16
12325	2	Flaps ∅ 16
12326	1	Front wheel complete
12327	1	Rear wheel complete
12336	1	Front hub complete ∅ 105
12336/1	1	Cover
1441/2	6	Nut
12336/2	1	Spacer ≠ 3
1441/4	1	Pin
12336/3	1	Hub body
1441/6	20	Front ball
1441/7	4	Cone
1441/8	2	Cap
1441/9	2	Dust cover
1442/8	2	Pairs of shoes with sole
1442/9	4	Spring

INDIAN-CLYMER MOTORCYCLE DIVISION	GROUP — CONTROLS AND WHEELS	Page No 32
	Refer to: (Photo No. 14 Page No. 34)	

Part number	No. Pcs.	DESCRIPTION
1441/12	2	Spinner
1441/14	2	Lever
1441/15	2	Clamp with nut and washer
1441/16	2	Nut
1441/17	2	Washer
1441/18	2	Adjuster
1441/19	4	Nut
1441/20	4	Washer
12337	1	Rear hub complete ⌀ 105
12337/1	1	Cover
1515/4	1	Pin
1442/4	1	Rear hub body
1442/5	22	Ball 7/32"
1442/6	2	Cap
1442/7	2	Dust-cover
12237/2	1	Rear wheel sprocket 60T.
1442/11	5	Bolt fixing sprocket
1442/12	1	Fixing sprocket plate
1442/13	5	Nut
12326/1	2	Wheel rim 16x44
12326/2	72	Spoke ⌀ 2,5
1435/3	72	Nipples ⌀ 2,5
12328	1	Spring
12331	1	Chain 105 links
684	2	Clip
11050/1	2	Clip fixing coil
11050	1	Outer ignition coil
11051	1	Plug pipe
8071	2	Rubber pipe
8041	2	Rubber
12303	1	Rear brake lever
692	1	Spacer

INDIAN-CLYMER MOTORCYCLE DIVISION	GROUP CONTROLS AND WHEELS Refer to: (Photo No. 14 Page No. 34)	Page No. 33

Part number	No. Pcs.	DESCRIPTION
693	2	Cables guard
985/1	1	Coil cable
12332	1	Engine cable
12336	1	Spark plug cable
11049	1	Cable-way

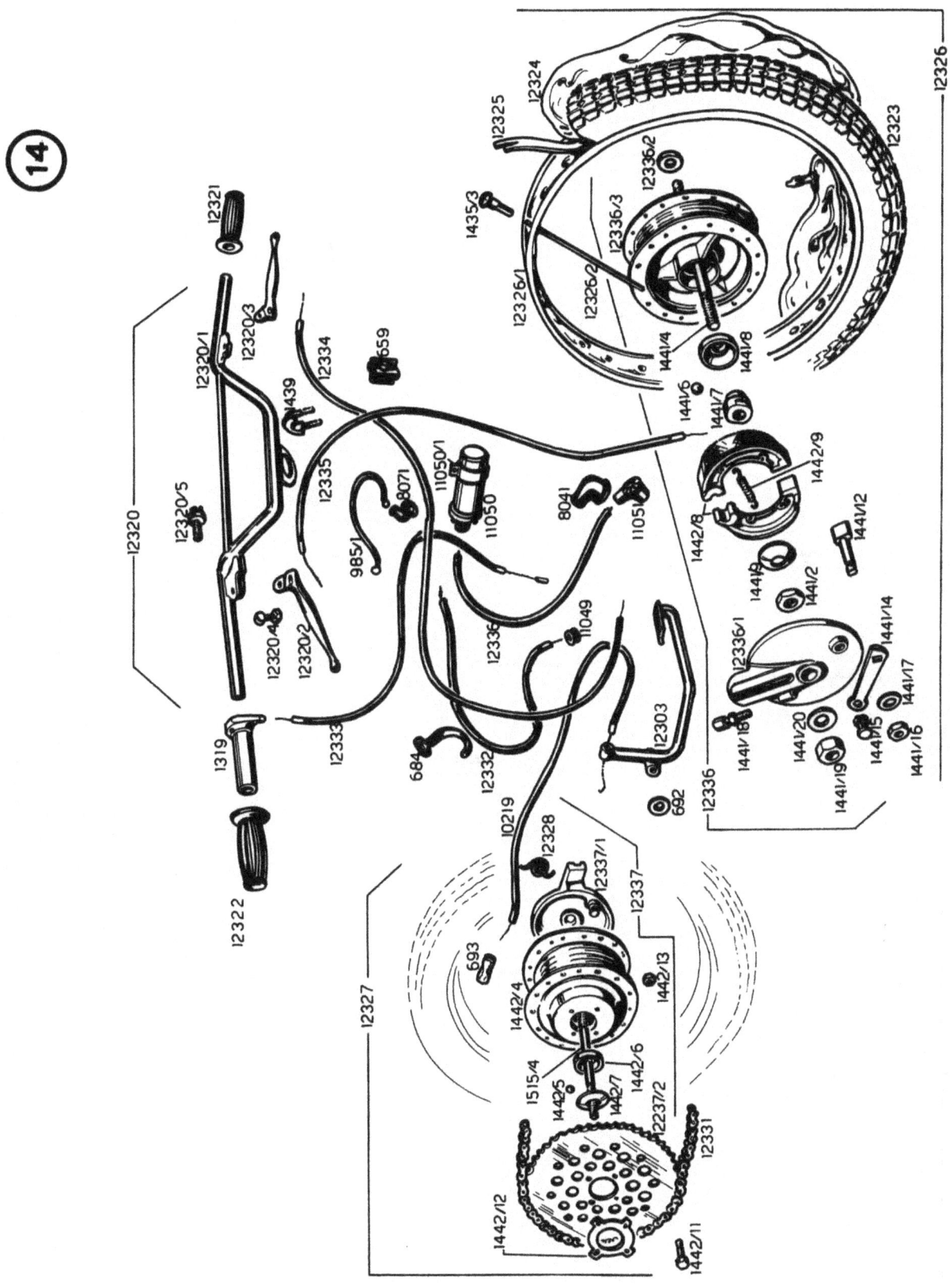

INDIAN-CLYMER MOTORCYCLE DIVISION

GROUP: CRANKCASE

Refer to: (Photo No. 15   Page No. 37)

Page No. 35

Refer. No.	Part number	No. Pcs.	DESCRIPTION
1	20 - 1122	1	Crankcase with bushes
1a	20 - 1123	1	Crankcase with bearings
2	359 - 11 - 121	1	Bush
3	550 - 11 - 212	1	Bush
4	20 - 1130	1	R.H. cover complete
5	6111312189	1	Screw
6	6111312191	2	Screw
7	20 - 1141	1	L.H. cover
8	351 - 11 - 201	1	Plug
9	792	2	Gasket
10	6111462100	1	Screw
11	150 - 11 - 061	1	Gasket
12	05 - 1116	1	Stud
13	6117011084	4	Washer
14	6111352075	6	Screw
15	359 - 11 - 033	1	Seal under L.H. cover
16	611131217	6	Screw
17	6111332104	3	Screw
18	05 - 1105	1	Cylinder barrel gasket
19	359 - 11 - 031	4	Bolt
20	6114012006	4	Nut
21	6117011064	4	Washer
22	555 - 11 - 007	2	Dowel bush
23	6146336004/C3	1	Ball bearing
24	982	2	Gasket
25	359 - 11 - 132	1	Gasket
26	614637636303/C3	2	Ball bearing
27	6146366202/C3	2	Ball bearing
28	6129310035	1	Circlip
29	6111312113	2	Screw
30	6129310042	1	Circlip
31	6111032169	1	Screw

INDIAN-CLYMER MOTORCYCLE DIVISION		GROUP CRANKCASE Refer to: (Photo No. 15 Page No. 37)		Page No 36

Refer. No.	Part number	No. Pcs.	DESCRIPTION
32	353 - 11 - 114	1	Gasket
33	05 - 1117	1	Crankcase gasket
34	05 - 1115	1	Cocer
35	793	2	Ring rubber
36	20 - 1137	1	Cower
38	20 - 1133	1	Washer
39	20 - 1132	1	Ring
40	781	1	Gasket
41	977	1	Ring
42	20 - 1136	1	Cower
43	6111552069	3	Screw
44	20 - 1113	2	Dowel bush
45	20 - 1114	1	Dowel bush
46	20 - 1138	1	Gasket
47	11049	1	Grommet

page n. 37

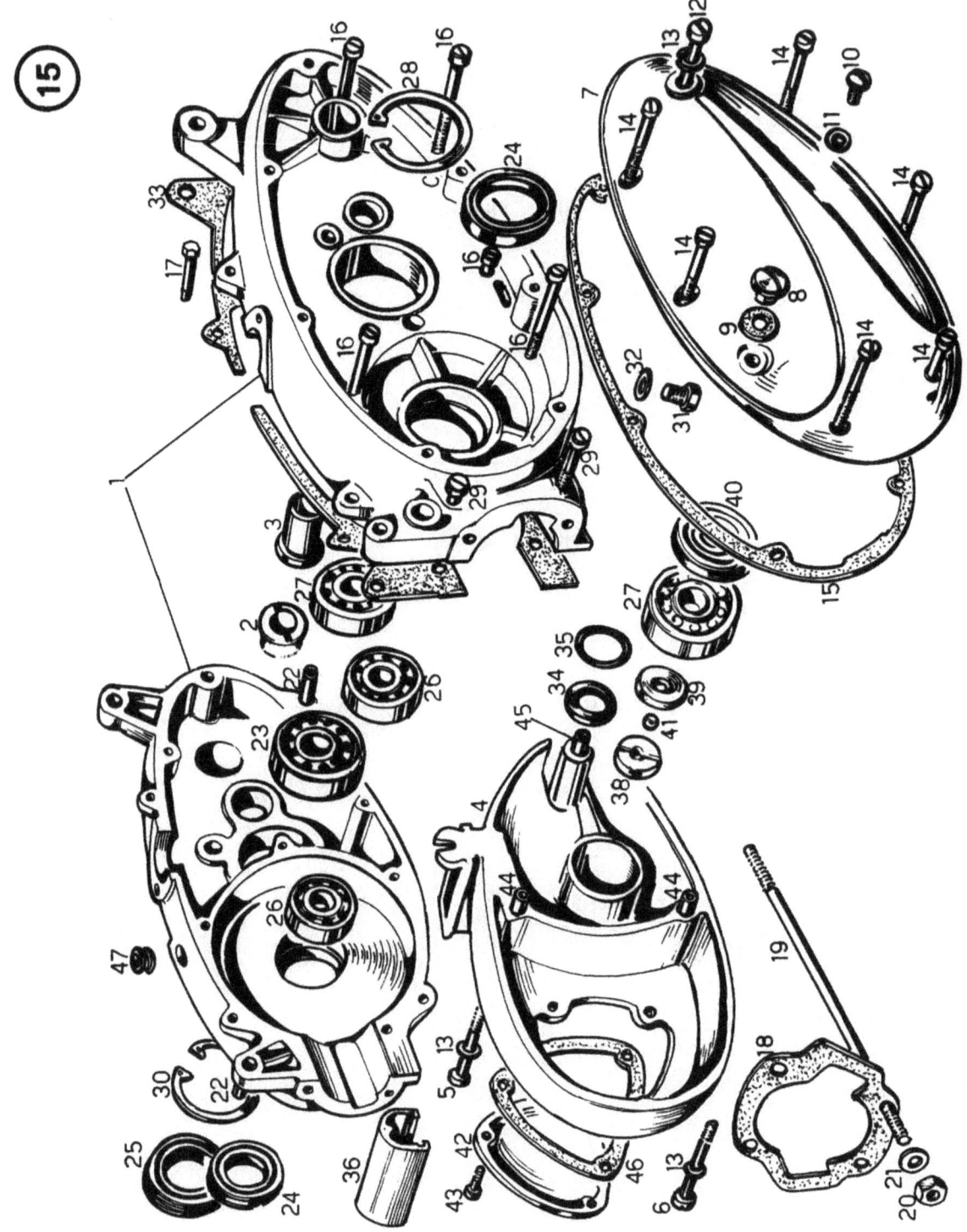

| | INDIAN-CLYMER MOTORCYCLE DIVISION | | GROUP COMPLETE CONNECTING ROD Refer to: (Photo No. 16 Page No. 40) | Page No 38 |

Refer. No.	Part number	No. Pcs.	DESCRIPTION
1	20 - 1205	1	Crankshaft and connecting rod
2	20 - 1207	1	R.H. crankshaft
3	20 - 1208	1	L.H. crankshaft
4	20 - 1225	1	Piston
-	20 - 1226		Piston 1st rebore
-	20 - 1227		Piston 2nd rebore
-	20 - 1228		Piston 3rd rebore
-	20 - 1229		Piston 4th rebore
5	353 - 12 - 014	3	Piston ring
-	359 - 12 - 015		Piston ring 1st rebore
-	359 - 12 - 016		Piston ring 2nd rebore
-	359 - 12 - 017		Piston ring 3rd rebore
-	359 - 12 - 018		Piston ring 4th rebore
6	05 - 1221	1	Gudgeon pin
7	05 - 1222	2	Wire circlip
8	05 - 1223	1	Sprocket
9	6117400122	1	Washer
10	6114030112	1	Nut
11	355 - 12 - 033	1	Securing peg
12	05 - 1232	1	Bush
13	05 - 1261	1	Connecting rod with pin and roller

	INDIAN-CLYMER MOTORCYCLE DIVISION		GROUP CYLINDER COMPLETE Refer to: (Photo No. 17 Page No. 40)	Page No 39

Refer. No.	Part number	No. Pcs.	DESCRIPTION
1	20 - 1400	1	Cylinder complete
2	359 - 13 - 013	1	Bush
3	20 - 1404	1	Cylinder head
4	6111781104	2	Fastening screw
5	6111781073	2	Fastening screw
6	14 - 8 - RZ	1	Spark plug

page n. 40

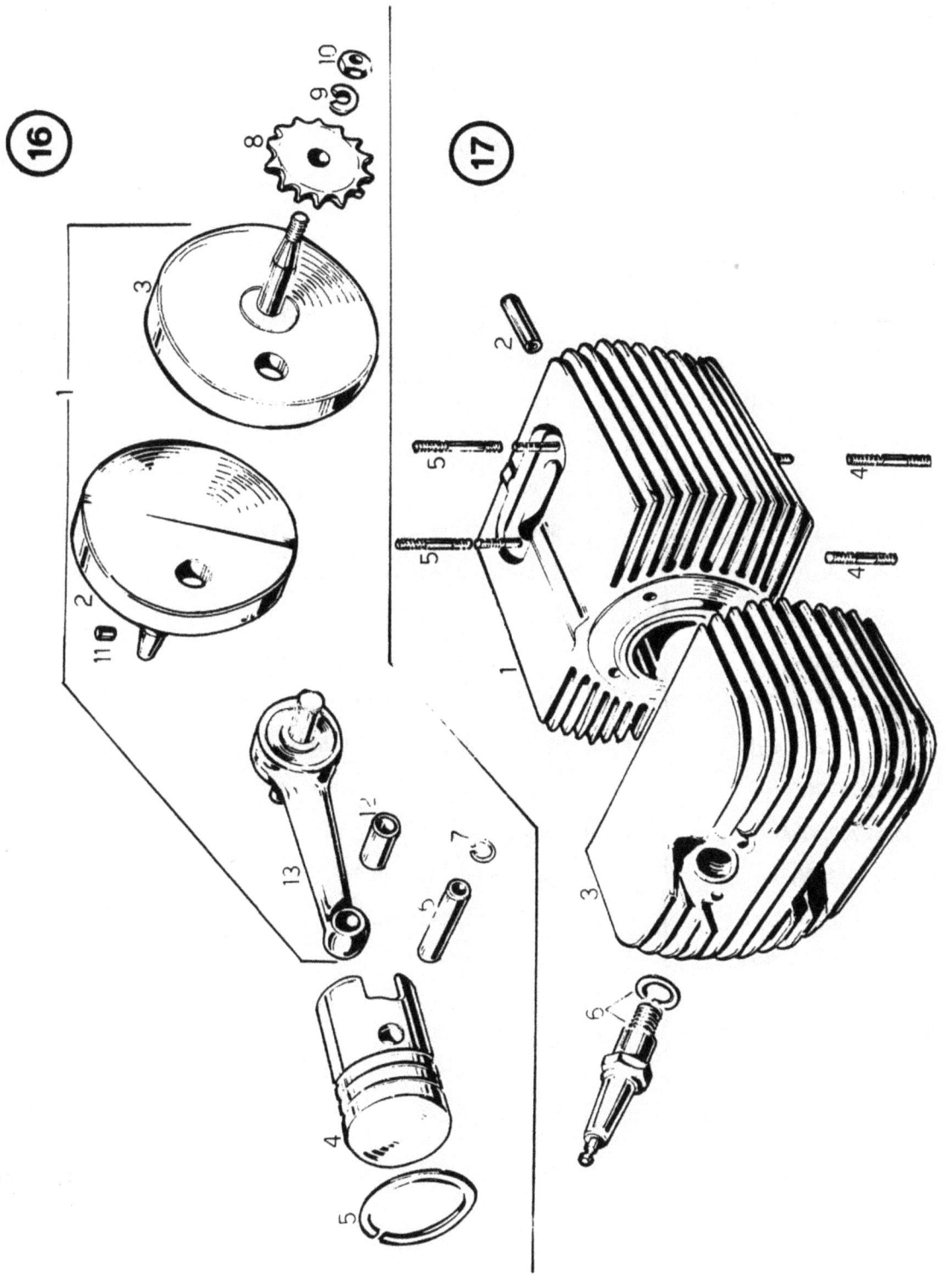

| INDIAN-CLYMER MOTORCYCLE DIVISION | GROUP GEAR-BOX AND KICK STARTER GEARS Refer to: (Photo No. 18   Page No. 42) | | Page No 41 |

Refer. No.	Part number	No. Pcs.	DESCRIPTION
1	20 - 2220	1	Main shaft
2	20 - 2222	1	Lay shaft
3	20 - 2205	1	1st gear 13T., 24T.
4	20 - 2223	1	2nd gear 20T.
5	20 - 2213	1	Driving gear with hub 23T.
6	359 - 22 - 037	1	Ring
7	550 - 22 - 050	1	Gearbox sprocket 13T.
8	555 - 56 - 302	1	Nut
9	20 - 2232	1	Circlip
10	20 - 2216	1	Speedometer shaft
11	05 - 2227	1	Kick starter ratchet with pin
12	20 - 2229	1	2nd gear 18T.
13	550 - 22 - 046	1	Kick starter spring
14	550 - 22 - 030	1	Kick starter pedal complete
15	359 - 22 - 038	1	Kick starter pedal key
16	6114013006	1	Nut
17	6117012064	1	Washer
20	20 - 2215	1	Ratchet with shaft
21	550 - 22 - 031	1	Kick starter pedal
22	150 - 22 - 050	1	Pedal
23	150 - 22 - 053	1	Pedal rubber
24	150 - 22 - 051	1	Spring
25	150 - 22 - 052	1	Washer
26	151 - 22 - 051	1	Circlip
27	6121500455	1	Peg

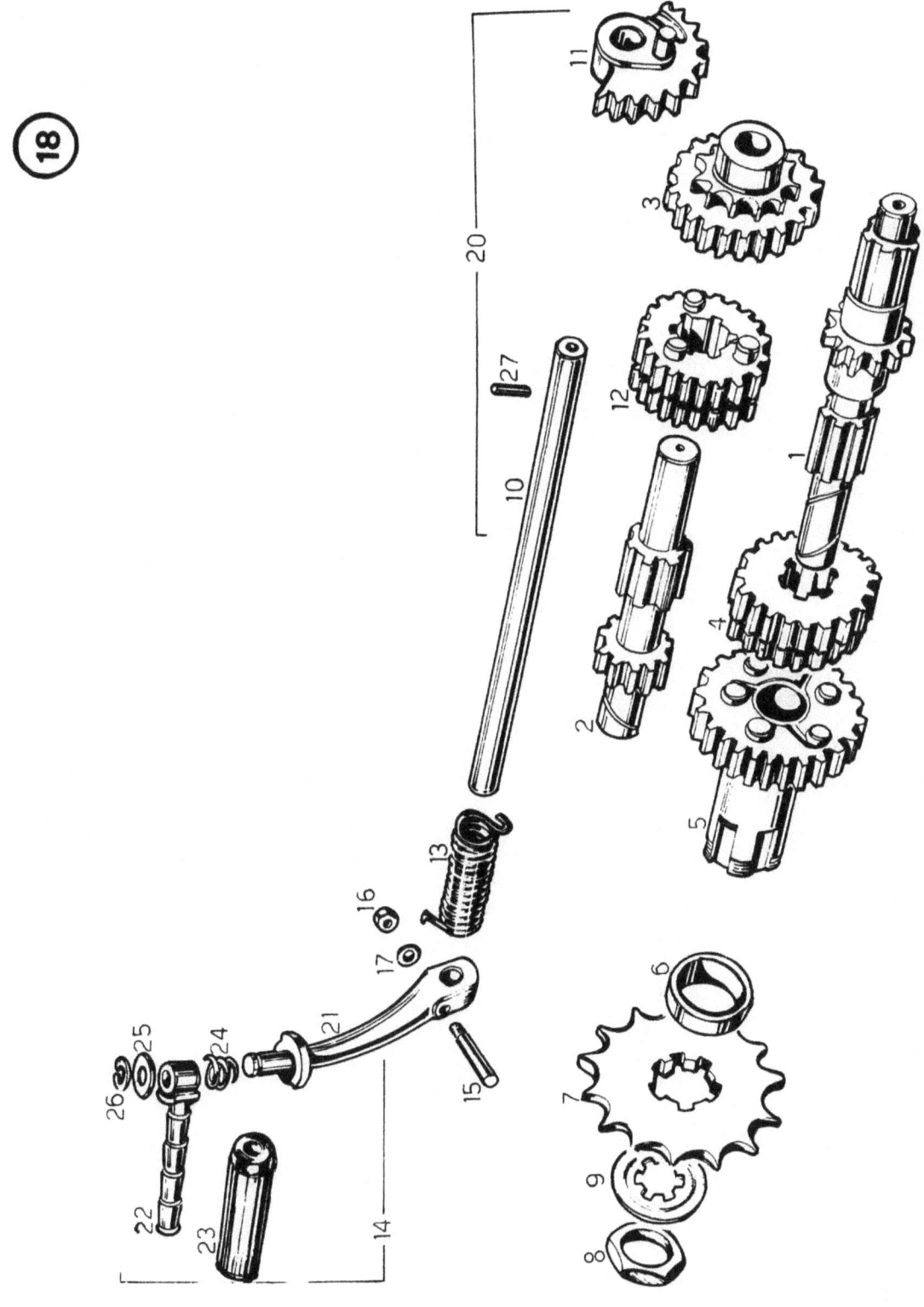

| | INDIAN-CLYMER MOTORCYCLE DIVISION | | GROUP SELECTOR AND GEAR Refer to: (Photo No. 19 Page No. 45) | Page No. 43 |

Refer. No.	Part number	No. Pcs.	DESCRIPTION
1	20 - 2410	1	Foot gear change mechanism
2	555 - 24 - 032	2	Spring
3	359 - 24 - 010	1	Fork complete
4	20 - 2403	1	Guide
6	355 - 24 - 012	1	Pedal rubber
7	05 - 2118	1	Rod
8	550 - 24 - 135	1	Spring
9	550 - 10 - 012	1	Screw
10	6111332104	1	Screw
11	6117402061	1	Washer
12	6129290009	1	Securing ring
13	20 - 2405	1	Gear change pedal welded
14	05 - 2128	1	Pin - welded
15	05 - 2127	1	Insert
16	6114011008	1	Nut
17	6117401082	1	Washer
18	6129290006	1	Circlip
19	6117012084	1	Washer

| | INDIAN-CLYMER MOTORCYCLE DIVISION | GROUP CLUTCH Refer to: (Photo No. 20   Page No. 45) | Page No 44 |

Refer. No.	Part number	No. Pcs.	DESCRIPTION
1	05 - 2101	2	Clutch chainwheel complete
2	05 - 2104	1	Fixed plate complete
3	05 - 2108	1	Pressure plate complete
4	05 - 2111	1	Plate
5	05 - 2112	5	Spring
6	05 - 2113	5	Cup
7	359 - 28 - 043	5	Washer
8	6129290004	6	Securing ring
9	05 - 2116	1	Circlip
10	05 - 2114	1	Nut
11	05 - 2115	1	Clutch operating rod
12	359 - 28 - 013	32	Cork insert
13	828	1	Primary chain 3/8x3/8 in. 44 links
14	6136800005	3	Ball
15	20 - 2125	1	Clutch operating rod
16	20 - 2121	1	Operating lever
17	20 - 2124	1	Lever pin
18	20 - 2123	1	Grub screw
19	6114032006	2	Nut

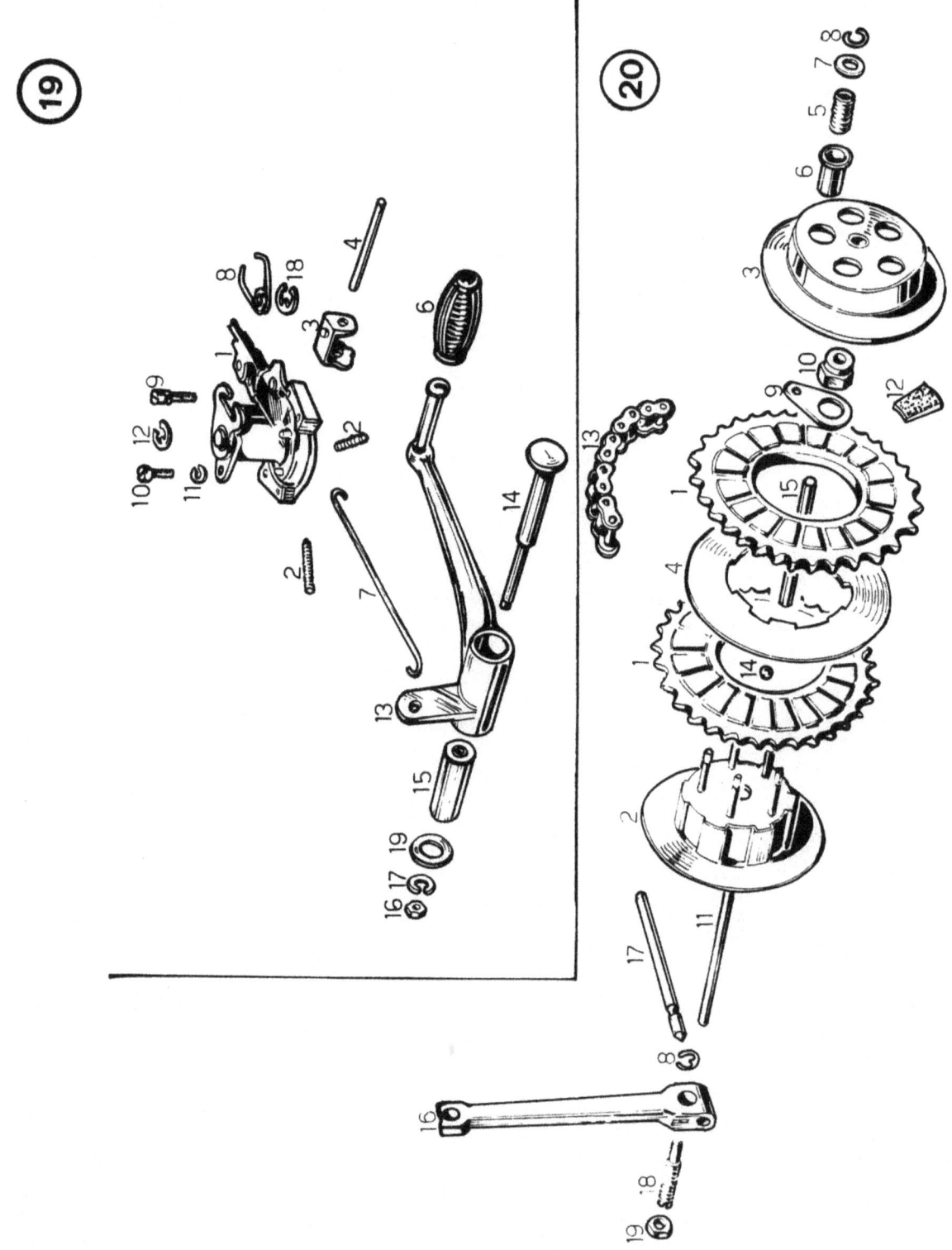

INDIAN-CLYMER MOTORCYCLE DIVISION	GROUP FLYWHEEL Refer to: (Photo No.21 Page No. 47)	Page No 46

Refer. No.	Part number	No. Pcs.	DESCRIPTION
1	05 - 6120	1	Magneto complete
2	05 - 6128	1	Stator body with wiper
3	05 - 6127	1	Condenser bracket
4	6123010287	1	Rivet
5	05 - 6132	1	Illuminative pole complete
6	05 - 6154	1	Ignition pole complete
7	05 - 6143	1	Numeral pole complete
8	05 - 6170	1	Dynamo rotor
9	05 - 6125	1	Cam
10	6111052083	1	Screw
11	6111312042	2	Screw
12	6111312048	4	Screw
13	6117402051	3	Washer
14	05 - 6105	1	Condenser
15	6111312076	2	Screw
16	359 - 61 - 012	2	Rest
17	355 - 61 - 230	1	Felt
18	6123011205	1	Rivet
19	355 - 61 - 240	1	Contact holder complete
20	355 - 61 - 260	1	Contact breaker arm
21	355 - 61 - 211	2	Insulation washer
22	6117332041	1	Washer
23	355 - 61 - 212	1	Insulation washer
24	6111032040	1	Screw
25	6111312039	1	Screw
26	6114012004	1	Nut
27	6117402043	7	Washer
28	355 - 61 - 214	1	Washer
29	05 - 6124	1	Connector

page n. 47

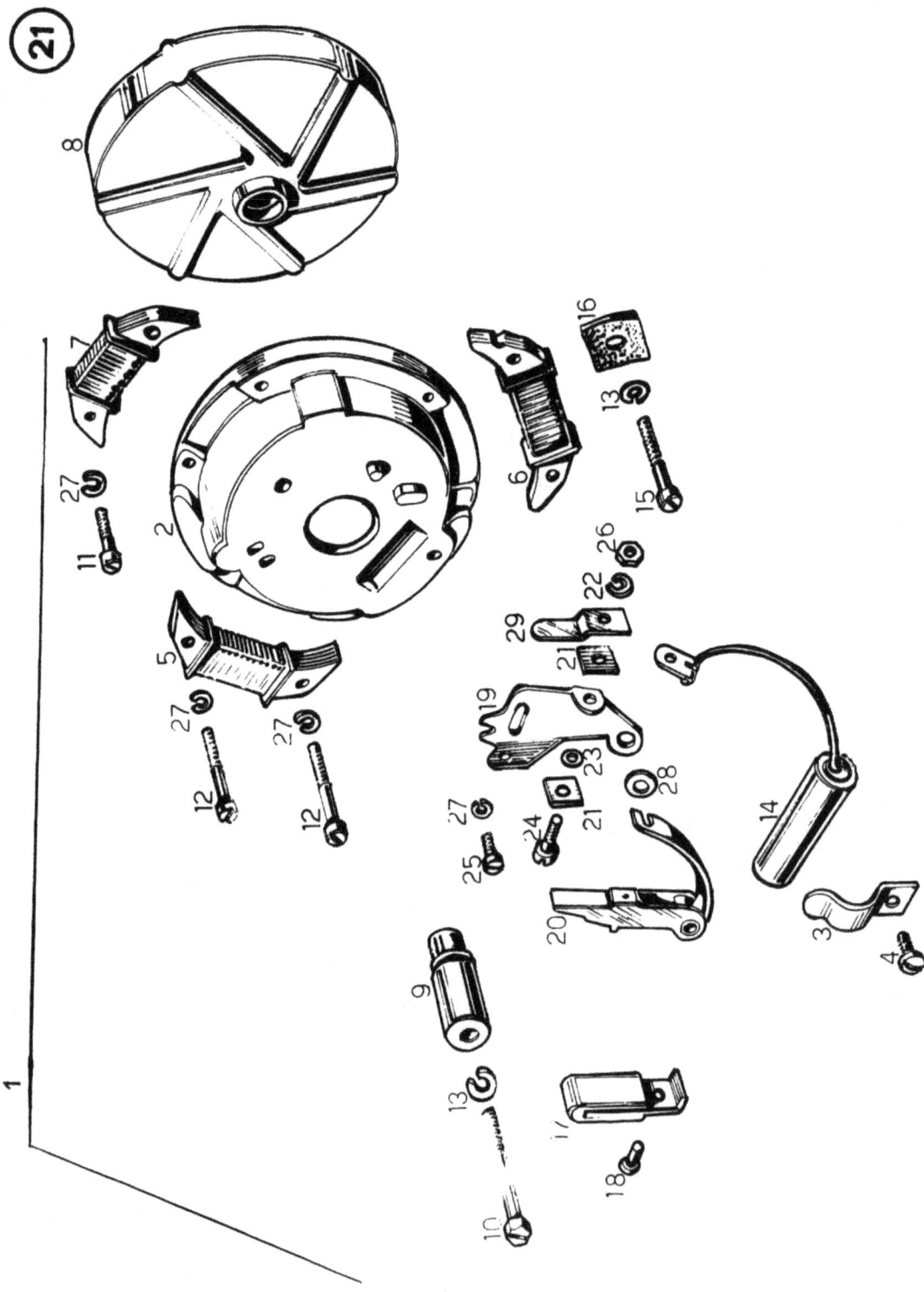

INDIAN-CLYMER MOTORCYCLE DIVISION		**GROUP** CARBURETTOR SHA 14/14 Refer to: (Photo No. 22 Page No. 50)	Page No 48

Refer. No.	Part number	No. Pcs.	DESCRIPTION
	1104 - 37	1	Top screw
	1486.60.02	1	Main jet
	1691.27	1	Nut
	2838.05	1	Needle
	3318.36	2	Top screw
	3346.61	1	Throttle valve spring
	3385.30	1	Gasket
	3598.36	2	Screw
	3606.61	1	Spring dia
	4190.36	1	Screw
	4560.22	1	Pin
	4611.50	1	Clamp
	4617.36	1	Screw
	5417.22	1	Screw
	6105.61	1	Spring
	6107.96	1	Float chamber
	6108.01.64	1	Throttle valve
	6109.29	1	Filter
	6110.53	1	Float chamber top
	6111.30	1	Seal under
	6112.26	1	Lever
	6114.50.64	1	Valve
	6115.22	1	Pin
	6117.86	1	Filter
	6122.01.80	1	Float complete
	6123.30	1	Seal under
	6140.37	1	Throttle valve adjusting screw
	6159.30	1	Seal ring dia
	6259.61	1	Spring dia
	6304.27	1	Nut
	6305.36	1	Screw
	6448.69	1	Seal ring

| INDIAN-CLYMER MOTORCYCLE DIVISION | GROUP CARBURETTOR SHA 14/14 Refer to: (Photo No. 22 Page No. 50) | Page No. 49 |

Refer. No.	Part number	No. Pcs.	DESCRIPTION
	6105.38	1	Pipe
	7204.85	1	Cap

page n. 50

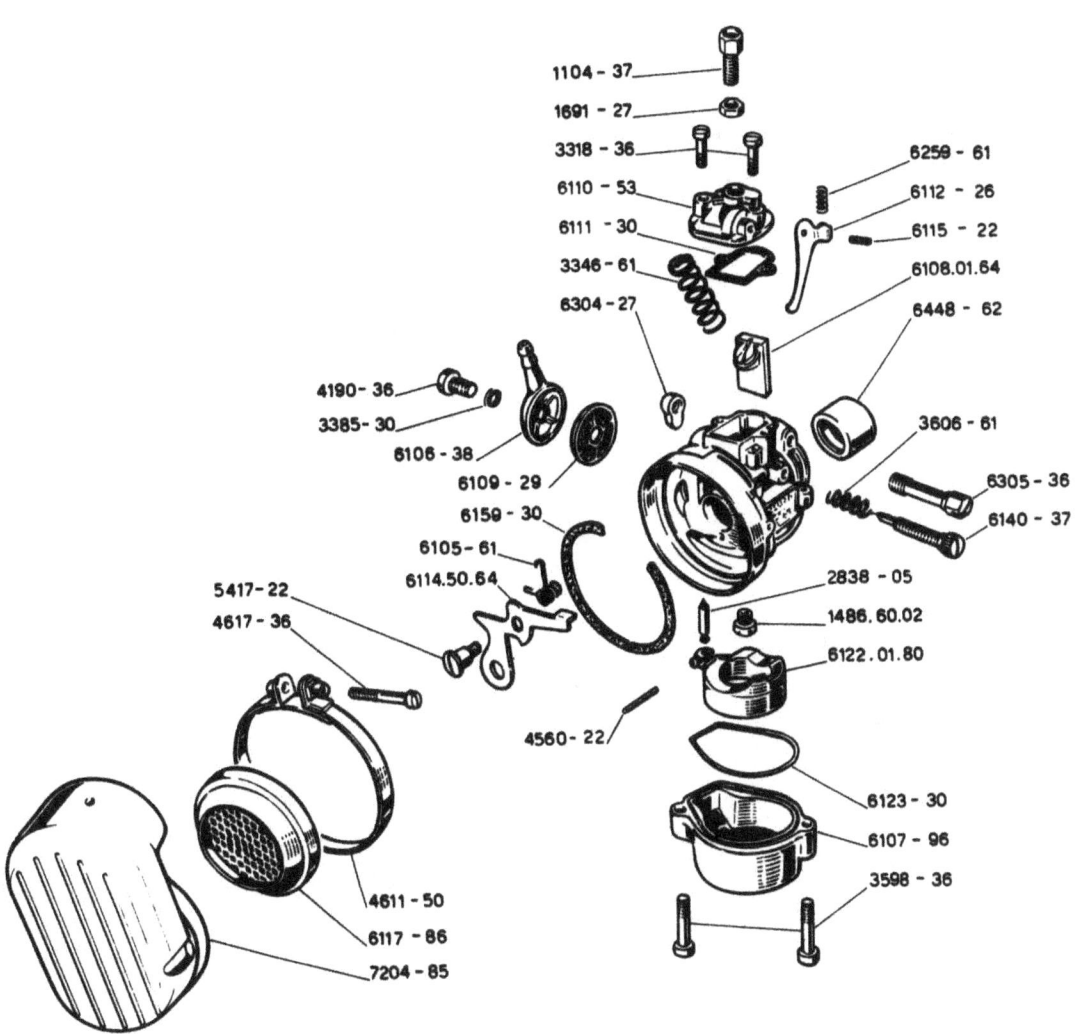

NOTES

PAPOOSE

Sales Literature Scrap Book
Pages 77 to 90

Illustrated Parts List
Pages 91 to 112

CLYMER PAPOOSE

ENGINE
Type	single cylinder, two cycle
Bore and stroke	38.8mm x 42mm
Displacement	49.6cc
Compression ratio	10.0 to 1
Max. horsepower	4.9 at 8,000 rpm
Ignition	flywheel magneto
Carburetion	one 19mm U.A. Dell'Orto
Lubrication	oil in gas

DIMENSIONS
Length	60 inches
Seat height	25 inches
Wheelbase	45 inches
Ground clearance	6.2 inches
Dry weight	130 pounds

BRAKES
Front brake	single leading shoe
Rear brake	single leading shoe
Tires	choice of trail or street

TRANSMISSION
Type	4-speed, foot operated
Clutch	wet, multi plate
Primary drive	gear

PERFORMANCE
Indicated highest one-way speed	47 mph
Acceleration 0-60	none
Braking distance 30-0	31 feet

FRAME AND SUSPENSION
Front suspension	telehydraulic fork
Rear suspension	hydraulic shock
Frame type	tubular backbone

COLORS -- red, blue
PRICE AS TESTED -- $345.00

DISTRIBUTOR
Floyd Clymer, Motorcycle Division
222 N. Virgil Ave.
Los Angeles, Calif.

PLEASE FILL IN, DETACH HERE AND MAIL TO US — RUSH ORDER BLANK

MAIL TO: Floyd Clymer, Motorcycle Division
222 No. Virgil Ave., Los Angeles, Calif. 90004

DATE _____

PLEASE SEND: _____ Indian Ponybike (3-speed). Lights & speedometer included . . . $295.00.
State color, red or gold _____. Trail or regular rear tire _____

_____ Indian Papoose (4-speed). Lights & speedometer included . . . $345.00
State color, red or blue _____. Road tires only available.

_____ Indian Boy Racer. No lights or speedometer. $325.00
Color blue and white only.

I enclose $_____ check or money order. Prices are F.O.B. Los Angeles. Deduct 3% for full remittance with order.

Age group _____ 10-15; _____ 15-20; _____ 20-30; _____ Over 30. Where did you first hear about new Indians? _____ Magazine? _____ Clymer direct mail? _____ Dealer? Thank you.

NAME _____

ADDRESS _____

CITY _____ STATE _____ ZIP _____

Indian: PONYBIKE AND PAPOOSE

One little, two little fifties from the Clymer-Munch tribe...

ONE LITTLE, two little... Ah, it's well known that there exist Zuni, Arapaho, Yavapi and Umatilla. But, Clymer-Munch is a relative newcomer among the names on the tribal roll. And, Papoose and Ponybike are the braves of that latter tribe.

Floyd Clymer, long-time two-wheel entrepeneur, Freidel Munch, West Germany's Mammothman, and assorted British, Italian and Czechoslovakian representatives of manufacturers of proprietary motorcycle, moped and minibike components have commingled to produce machinery, escalating from 50 cc, through mid-range displacements, to the mammoth 1000-cc Mammoth. The 50-cc segment includes the aforementioned Papoose and Ponybike.

This pair of machines can be classed as belonging to one of two categories—small, vest pocket motorcycle, or large, overdressed minibike. Both are distributed through franchised dealers by Floyd Clymer's Motorcycle Division, Los Angeles, Calif.

The Ponybike and Papoose share a number of features. Both are equipped with telescopic forks and swinging arm rear suspension; both are equipped with

CYCLE WORLD IMPRESSION

full (magneto type) lighting; both are fitted with internal expanding brakes, front and rear. Beyond this, the similarities become a bit broader, and outright differences begin to appear.

The Ponybike is based on a single truss frame. The 50-cc Jawa/CZ two-stroke engine is suspended beneath this single downtube from a pair of welded-on plates, stamped deeply for stiffening. The Czech powerplant, on 9:1 compression, develops 4.8 bhp at 8000 rpm. Power is delivered through a gear primary drive, through a three-speed gearbox and multi-disc wet clutch, to a single-row chain final drive.

The Papoose, on the other hand, is powered by a B.F. Minarelli engine of 49.6-cc piston displacement and 10:1 compression. Likewise, the 4.19-bhp engine, which also peaks at 8000 rpm, has a gear primary drive. However, the gearbox is a four-speed unit. The Papoose's clutch also is a multi-plate, wet assembly; and, final drive is by single-row chain. The engine-gearbox is suspended from a single downtube by an inverted-U yoke arrangement.

Both engines operate on regular grade fuel, with a 20:1 oil-in-fuel mix. Both employ magneto ignition and folding crank kick starters.

The machines investigated and ridden by CYCLE WORLD crewmen both showed a degree of workmanship and attention to detail not found on the domestic minibike.

Paint on the fire engine red Papoose and the bronze, gold and white Ponybike appeared flawless.

Cables, clutch and brake levers (ball end on the Papoose, blade end on the Ponybike), lighting equipment, and handlebar grips all are recognizable as items drawn from that vast well of motorcycle components that is Italy. These things complete the slick, finished aura of the Clymer superminis, as compared with the rough welded, backyard mechanicals of the domestic product.

Performance of the Ponybike and Papoose are indistinguishable one from the other. Both approach the 50-mph mark for top speed. Both exhibit the excessively quick steering that is directly associated with small diameter wheels, though the control ratio isn't as abrupt, say, as with the 6-in. wheels of the true minibike. Both machines go well on pavement and on hard off-road surfaces. In sand, unfortunately, neither the Jawa/CZ nor the Minarelli engine is capable of sufficient torque delivery to permit continued progress. In sand, unfortunately, these machines invariably bog down to stay. The Ponybike is offered with optional block tread tires. These would do little, without sufficient power to make the added traction worthwhile.

List price of either machine is in the $300 bracket—something more than the average minibike, something less than the average motorcycle, which is what the Papoose or Ponybike buyer expects for his money. And, this purchaser, in addition to acquiring one of the cutest of the sub-motorcycle range, also will acquire title to that once-magic, ever-nostalgic name, Indian.

AMERICA'S MOST POPULAR COMEDIANS
ROWAN and MARTIN

ARE INDIAN "PAPOOSE" OWNERS

LAUGH-IN IS THEIR FAMOUS TV SHOW

Floyd Clymer teaches Dan Rowan how to ride his new "Papoose."

Dick Martin as the Werewolf in the "Maltese Bippy."

REPRINTED from

MODERN CYCLE

THE INDIAN PAPOOSE
A LITTLE MEMBER OF A GROWING TRIBE.

Not too long ago kids rode mini-bikes and adults rode motorcycles. The Mini was too small for the adult to ride in comfort and kids couldn't even get on a motorcycle. Lately a new breed of machine has come along, a machine that looks like a mini-bike, yet offers characteristics usually found on full size motorcycles. The "maxi-mini" retains the general shape of its smaller cousin, while, at the same time, delivering performance that can keep an adult happy. One of the newest of these machines is called the Indian Papoose and it comes from the growing Floyd Clymer tribe.

The Papoose is the sort of machine you would take places you wouldn't consider going on a mini-bike. It's got a good form of suspension, it's light and easily horsed over obstacles and, because of its configuration, you never feel called upon to prove anything to anyone in the speed department. Don't get us wrong, the Clymer Papoose will scoot along at a nice clip, it's just that, as far as we're concerned, you never feel called upon to prove anything to another rider on his hot trail bike.

A single cylinder, two cycle Minarelli engine provides the power that moves the Papoose. Induction is controlled by the movement of the piston and the compression ratio is a brisk 10 to 1. The bore of the cylinder is 38.8mm and the stroke is 42mm. A little work with conversion chart and pencil will show that these figures give a total capacity of 49.6cc. A maximum 4.9 horsepower develops at 8,000 revolutions per minute and the spark for ignition is developed by a flywheel magneto. The light alloy head and iron barrel are carried on cast alloy engine cases. Sharing space in the cases is a four speed constant mesh transmission. A 19mm Dellorto carburetor feeds the fuel to the combustion chamber and a two piece exhaust pipe carried on the right side of the machine gets rid of the spent gasses. A chrome plated perforated heat shield keeps the rider's leg from coming in contact with the hot pipe.

Primary drive between the crankshaft and the clutch mechanism is by gear and the multi plate clutch turns in a wet bath. The shift lever is mounted on the left side of the machine and the pattern is: down for low then up with the toe for the rest of the speeds. The shift lever is typically Italian; that's to say it's of the treadle variety. It can be actuated with pressure from the heel. After spending some time on the machine you begin to appreciate this much maligned type of shift lever.

The Papoose is a cold blooded little devil and requires much time on the choke when starting from cold. The choke is a simple plunger device with the control protruding from the left side of the carburetor. The willing little Minarelli mill is fastened to the frame at two places at the rear of the cases and a hanger from the backbone tube is bolted to the cylinder head. The fact that the Papoose doesn't have a fast top speed doesn't mean that it lacks pep. Good quantities of torque are available and it's no big thing to loft the front wheel when moving off the line in low gear. The machine starts easily, and, once warmed up, it seems willing, and able, to climb almost any size obstacle.

One of the features that make the Papoose such an able performer is the relatively large tires the bike comes equipped with. Mini-bikes are plagued with the problem of their little wheels falling into potholes and ruts. The larger wheels on the Indian are more suited to mildly rough terrain. The 45 inch wheelbase comes close to the dimensions found on several trail bikes and the dry weight of 110 pounds accounts for the ease with

Movement of the front forks is limited, but what action there is does a surprisingly good job of damping the jolts. Both brakes are housed in full width finned hubs.

which the machine can be horsed over obstacles.

Both tires come with what might be called a modified road tread pattern and both are laced to full width finned hubs. Bowden cables are used to actuate the binders and stopping power is fully up to the demands made by the machine. Usually we would want tires with a little more "bite" but in the case of the Papoose the standard tires proved to be up to the job. Ground clearance is 6.2 inches; that sounds a little short until you remember that a couple of moto cross machines on the market don't offer much more in the way of clearance. One bad feature is that the engine cases are completely exposed. Some sort of skid plate should be made available for the machine.

Suspension, frequently non-existant on a mini-bike, is surprisingly good on the Papoose. Springing at the rear of the machine is handled by a pair of dampers that look like those found on full sized motorcycles. The exposed chrome plated springs add a racy appearance to the aft section of the bike. The

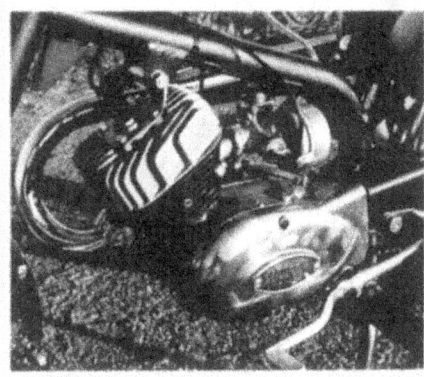

Power for the Papoose is provided by a 50cc three speed unit construction engine built by Minarelli. The carburetor is supplied with plunger-type choke which we found to be very useful when starting from cold.

front forks are totally enclosed in metal shrouding in an attempt to keep dirt and moisture from reaching places where they're not wanted. Movement at the front end is rather limited but not so much as to offer a rough ride. At the pace at which the Papoose is intended to go the suspension proves to be more than adequate.

Holding the Papoose together is a double backbone tube frame. A large diameter tube descends from the steering head and curves to a point aft of the engine. A smaller diameter tube connects the steering head and the nose of the sub-frame and also suports the gastank. This type of configuration is light and sturdy. All welds are nicely dressed and the metallic red paint is nicely applied.

Full lighting equipment is furnished with the Papoose, as are the

Rear suspension looks like something you'd find on a full size motorcycle. A plastic shroud carried inside the coil spring protects the damper rod from dirt and moisture.

other components necessary to make the machine street legal. We much prefer the Papoose as a dirt machine! In photographs the seat looks sparse, in use it proves to be very comfortable. The high handlebars bring the controls up to a point where an adult can operate them in comfort.

The Indian Papoose is available in either red or blue finish and retails for $345.00. It's not a full sized motorcycle, but it's much, much more than a mini. ☉

Two families of Apache Indians introduce their real live papooses to the Indian Papoose

Assembly line for Indian Papoose has a capacity of 100 units daily.

INDIAN PAPOOSE

Make a pet of a

PAPOOSE
— it'll grow on you

Reprint of
CYCLE GUIDE
ROAD TEST

THE MINI-BIKE has grown up... courtesy of Floyd Clymer's motorcycle division. His 'Papoose' might *look* like a mini-bike at first glance but just move a little closer.

The wheels are bigger than the mini-bikes we have been used to, the forks are longer, the frame is taller. In fact, the 'Papoose' is really a small motorcycle styled along 'mini' lines. Or as Floyd says, it's a SUPER mini-bike!

His nicety of definition is backed up by the all-round performance of the 'Papoose.' It will run up to around 50 mph, pulling wheelies in all four gears, it handles almost to big bike standards and is equally at home on street or trail!

Pushing the 'Papoose' into the SUPER mini-bike performance bracket is a 50cc Minarelli engine built in Italy and basically the same as the unit that

the Italian concern used to set a string of 50cc world speed records a couple of years ago.

A conventionally-ported two-stroke with four speed gearbox it produces 4.2 bhp and buzzes to 8,000 rpm. Its racing heritage shows in the centrally-mounted spark plug and the horizontal Del 'Orto carburetor with remote float chamber.

The exhaust pipe and muffler sweep,

CYCLE GUIDE

The sporty little Minarelli engine with central plug and horizontal carb.

The upswept trail-type exhaust pipe has a heat-shield to protect rider.

trail fashion, up along the right hand side of the bike with a metal heat shield keeping the rider's leg from getting third degree burns.

The muffler is a huge and really effective piece of equipment that dampens down the hornet's buzz exhaust note that is so often an annoying feature of tiny two-strokes.

Annoying features are things that the 'Papoose' just doesn't have. There is nothing about which you can really gripe and wail ... it may not be the most spectacular exciter in the world but it sets out to fill a hole in the market and does so admirably.

The seat is comfortable, the brakes work, the engine is zippy ... in a word, it's FUN.

Unless you're a budding Larry Bergquist the 'Papoose' is a great little performer in the dirt. Included in its purchase price of $345 are either street or trail tires ... whichever the customer prefers.

We'd go for the trail tires every time. Though it doesn't fold up (it's NOT a mini-bike, remember?) the Papoose is small enough to fit in a good-sized car trunk if the handlebar clamps are slackened off and the bars pushed down. And it's certainly not too heavy that it can't be hung on a set of those rear bumper bike racks.

So load it up and head for the boonies. On the street the 'Papoose' is just another tiny, rather slow motorbike. Out in the wilds it's a gas!

It will go anywhere that the average rider feels like taking it and where it won't make it you can carry it. Pick up thy 'Papoose' and walk!

Speedo calibrated to 70mph is built in Italy. Bike will hit almost 50mph

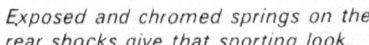

The front brake is of the single leading shoe type — most effective!

Exposed and chromed springs on the rear shocks give that sporting look.

Front telescopic forks and the swinging arm rear suspension both have enough travel for some pretty serious rock-bashing and the engine is lusty enough to cope with all but the steepest inclines. So for just pottering around the trails with a minimum of effort and at a fairly casual pace, the Papoose is fine.

The Minarelli engine has a bore and stroke of 38.8 mm by 42 mm and runs on a compression ratio of 10:1. Ignition is by flywheel magneto and it has coil lighting. Carburetion is by the Del 'Orto UA19S model and transmission is through a wet clutch.

No torque figures are available but the strong little motor has it in spades. Riding it was enough to prove that.

Gas mileage is up around 100 mpg ... as should be expected from a 50cc engine ... and this means that you can fill up the gas tank (just over a gallon) and forget all about it for a month or so.

All controls are just as on a regular motorcycle — rear brake operated by the right foot, rocking pedal gear change on the opposite side, clutch and brake levers on left and right handlebars respectively.

The general finish of the machine is excellent. It comes in either red or blue paintwork which is deep and well-applied. There is enough chrome plating to enhance the looks without mak-

The gas tank holds just over a gallon — enough for a hundred miles riding.

Front forks have enough travel to cope with pretty hefty rocks and gullies.

ing the bike appear grayish and the chrome is solid and of obvious good quality.

Completely exposed, chromed springs on the rear shock absorbers help with the sporty appearance as do the upswept cowhorn bars with knobby moto-cross type handlebar grips.

Chain adjustment is by a snail cam at the rear wheel spindle, a simple and foolproof way of ensuring correct chain tension. A neat point here is the serrated flat on the cam that makes it double-easy to push the cam around with one's thumb. Only a small detail point, maybe, but how much easier to operate than some chain adjustment cams that you have to bash around with a hammer and drift!

This is typical of the thought that has gone into the design and manufacture of the Papoose.

Other detail points pleasing to note are things like the sporting ball-ended control levers, the roomy toolbox beneath the seat and the lever-type petcock, so much more convenient than the push and pull type.

The ball-ended levers will particularly appeal to the trail riders. Most dirt riders get off occasionally and no-one relishes the thought of a sharp-ended control lever puncturing their skin!

So that's it ... the Indian Papoose bears one of the most respected and revered names in American motorcycling and it's as different as can be from those Indians of long ago. But that doesn't mean a thing, the design, the quality of production and the performance make the Papoose more than worthy of the Indian name.

The toolbox is mounted under the seat and is big enough to hold all tools needed for general running repairs.

Indian: PONYBIKE AND PAPOOSE
One little, two little fifties from the Clymer-Munch tribe

ONE LITTLE, two little... Ah, it's well known that there exist Zuni, Arapaho, Yavapi and Umatilla. But, Clymer-Munch is a relative newcomer among the names on the tribal roll. And, Papoose and Ponybike are the braves of that latter tribe.

This pair of machines can be classed as belonging to one of two categories—small, vest pocket motorcycle, or large, overdressed minibike. Both are distributed through franchised dealers by Floyd Clymer's Motorcycle Division, Los Angeles, Calif.

The Ponybike and Papoose share a number of features. Both are equipped with telescopic forks and swinging arm rear suspension; both are equipped with full (magneto type) lighting; both are fitted with internal expanding brakes, front and rear. Beyond this, the similarities become a bit broader, and outright differences begin to appear.

The Ponybike is based on a single truss frame. The 50-cc Jawa/CZ two-stroke engine is suspended beneath this single downtube from a pair of welded-on plates, stamped deeply for stiffening. The Czech powerplant, on 9:1 compression, develops 4.8 bhp at 8000 rpm. Power is delivered through a gear primary drive, through a three-speed gearbox and multi-disc wet clutch, to a single-row chain final drive.

The Papoose, on the other hand, is powered by a B.F. Minarelli engine of 49.6-cc piston displacement and 10:1 compression. Likewise, the 4.19-bhp engine, which also peaks at 8000 rpm, has a gear primary drive. However, the gearbox is a four-speed unit. The Papoose's clutch also is a multi-plate, wet assembly; and, final drive is by single-row chain. The engine-gearbox is suspended from a single downtube by an inverted-U yoke arrangement.

Both engines operate on regular grade fuel, with a 20:1 oil-in-fuel mix. Both employ magneto ignition and folding crank kick starters.

The machines investigated and ridden by CYCLE WORLD crewmen both showed a degree of workmanship and attention to detail not found on the domestic minibike.

Paint on the fire engine red Papoose and the bronze, gold and white Ponybike appeared flawless.

Cables, clutch and brake levers (ball end on the Papoose, blade end on the Ponybike), lighting equipment, and handlebar grips all are recognizable as items drawn from that vast well of motorcycle components that is Italy. These things complete the slick, finished aura of the Clymer superminis, as compared with the rough welded, backyard mechanicals of the domestic product.

Performance of the Ponybike and Papoose are indistinguishable one from the other. Both approach the 50-mph mark for top speed. Both exhibit the excessively quick steering that is directly associated with small diameter wheels, though the control ratio isn't as abrupt, say, as with the 6-in. wheels of the true minibike. Both machines go well on pavement and on hard off-road surfaces. In sand, unfortunately, neither the Jawa/CZ nor the Minarelli engine is capable of sufficient torque delivery to permit continued progress. In sand, unfortunately, these machines invariably bog down to stay. The Ponybike is offered with optional block tread tires. These would do little, without sufficient power to make the added traction worthwhile.

List price of either machine is in the $300 bracket—something more than the average minibike, something less than the average motorcycle, which is what the Papoose or Ponybike buyer expects for his money. And, this purchaser, in addition to acquiring one of the cutest of the sub-motorcycle range, also will acquire title to that once-magic, ever-nostalgic name, Indian.

INDIAN PONYBIKE

INDIAN PAPOOSE

THE RAYBORN FAMILY OWN AND RIDE INDIANS

CAL RAYBORN, winner Indianapolis, Daytona and other famous A.M.A. National Championships and one of the world's outstanding riders, uses his Indian Papoose for errands around the pits, at his home and other places. His youngsters and Mrs. Rayborn also ride Indians for sport, fun, recreation and health. Cal does not race Indians, but wins most of his races on a fast Harley-Davidson 45 cu. in. side valve V-twin — some on a Sprint. He has never raced on Indian — we wish he did. We salute Harley-Davidson for Rayborn's fine performances on their excellent bikes.

Cal takes his son riding. This youngster may be a national champion by 1990. He already rides his Indian like a "champ."

INDIAN DEALER FRANCHISES AVAILABLE

We have openings in many cities and towns where, with small capital, qualified persons can get started in a growing business.

Established dealers handling other lines will find Indian a valuable franchise to add to their present lines.

No charge for franchises. You only pay for merchandise to get started with Indian.

In small towns and rural districts we have openings for rider dealers. Good profit-making possibilities. Write us for details.

FLOYD CLYMER MOTORCYCLE DIVISION

222 N. Virgil Avenue • Los Angeles, California 90004
Phone: (213) 388-5119 • Cable: "Clymer" Los Angeles

MANUFACTURERS
Indian Motorcycles made in Italy

•

U.S. and Canadian distributors for
Clymer-Minarelli
cycle and minibike 2-stroke engines
and
Clymer-Tartarini Telescopic Forks
and
Royal-Enfield British Motorcycles
for all states west of Mississippi River

IMPORTANT NOTICE

SPECIAL OFFER!

These INDIANS are stylish, well designed and engineered, and beautifully finished with excellent paint jobs. They are actually small motorcycles or super (large) minibikes, yet small enough to fit easily into a station wagon, passenger car trunk (if handlebars are lowered), camper, truck, airplane, boat or mobile home.

Easier to ride and SAFER - They are easier riding and SAFER than most minibikes because they have speeds up to 50 mph, with a 2-stroke 50cc engine that performs more like a 90cc than a 50. Two brakes, front and rear, and full spring suspension make for E-Z riding and handling as they have wire spoke wheels and Pirelli tires (10 x 3.00 front, 10 x 3.50 rear - larger than most minibikes).

INDIAN, the oldest name in U. S. motorcycling, offers the following features, many of them exclusive, on these models:

PAPOOSE -- 4-speed, 50 mph, the best of our minis! Price is $345.00 F.O.B. Los Angeles, crated ready to ship, with regular road tires. Dual seat. Add $10.00 per wheel if you want knobby (trail) tires. Specify red or blue color.

PONYBIKE -- 3-speed, 50 mph, trail bike special. Price $295.00 crated ready to ship, with road tires and dual seat. Add $10.00 per wheel for knobby (trail) tires. Specify gold or red color.

Lights, front and rear, and speedometer included as standard equipment on Papoose and Ponybike models.

BOY RACER -- With 2.25 x 16" tires and wire spoke wheels. 50 mph. For kids 6 to 18 years of age. It's really too small for adults, as it is a real scaled down motorcycle, but not a toy. It's a practical bike. The larger-than-scooter wheels enables the rider to "broadside" on dirt corners just like a big bike. Specify red or blue color. $325.00. Add $10.00 per wheel if you want knobby (trail) tires. Has no lights or speedo, as it is strictly an off-the-road model.

INFORMATION ON ABOVE BIKES --

PRICES -- are F.O.B. our Los Angeles warehouse. Includes delivery to airport or freight office (either motor truck or rail).

World's Largest Publisher of Books on Autos, Motorcycles, Racing and Americana

SHIPPED COMPLETE -- Not in knocked down kit form. Packed one to a crate. Easy to set up. Only necessary to uncrate, attach handlebars and footpegs (about 20 minutes work), add mixture of regular gas and oil and you are ready to roll.

TERMS -- Cash. We have no time payment plan; however, buyer may deduct 3% cash discount if remittance is sent with order. If machines are sent C.O.D. or sight draft through a bank, the 3% discount does not apply - only if remittance is sent with order.

SPARE PARTS -- We have large stocks in Los Angeles. Almost overnight service to any U. S. location.

GUARANTEE -- 30 days or 1,000 miles, whichever comes first.

APPROXIMATE SHIPPING COSTS -- Machines weigh 99 to 106 lbs. Crated about 115 lbs. Motor truck is cheapest and charges run from $4.00 to $6.00 per machine to West Coast states (3 to 4 days arrival time); $12.00 to $14.00 to Mountain states (5 to 7 days arrival time); $15.00 to $16.00 to Midwest states (8 to 10 days arrival time); $18.00 to $20.00 to Eastern states and far South (12 to 14 days arrival time). You pay transportation upon arrival.

AIR SHIPMENTS - You may want air shipment, and air freight is very reasonable. Add about 50% of above estimates for air freight. Usually overnight delivery to large cities with airports suitable for jets. Another day or so if transfer is necessary for air or truck freight to small towns or cities with small airports. If you are near a large city, it is best and faster if we send directly to the airport, marked "HOLD FOR PICKUP" (example: Notify John Doe - phone POdunk 666-8888).

For instance, we shipped a Papoose to a Pontiac dealer, marked "hold for pickup at TWA office Pittsburgh, Pa." He drove 70 miles and had his bike at 9:00 A.M. the following morning. It would have taken two or three more days had it been transferred to a truck to haul 70 miles to his small town.

TITLE AND INSTRUCTIONS -- We send these by air mail when the bike is shipped. The "Certificate of Origin" is your bill of sale, and we include a paid invoice and instructions for setting up and operation.

Indian TECHNICAL DATA CHART

	PONYBIKE	BOY RACER	PAPOOSE
Engine:	Jawa M-23	Jawa M-23	Minarelli P4 "Sport"
Type:	Two-Stroke	Two-Stroke	Two-Stroke
No. of Cylinders:	One	One	One
Displacement:	50cc.	50cc.	50cc.
Bore:	38mm.	38mm.	38.8mm.
Stroke:	44mm.	44mm.	42mm.
Horsepower:	4.8	4.8	4.9
Compression Ratio:	9.0:1	9.0:1	9.0:1
Carburetor:	Jikov	Dellorto SHA 14.14	Dellorto UA19S
Fuel Capacity:	1.2 Gal.	1.2 Gal.	1.2 Gal.
Lubrication:	Gas/Oil Mixture	Gas/Oil Mixture	Gas/Oil Mixture
Clutch:	Multi. Disc in Oil	Multi. Disc in Oil	Multi. Disc in Oil
Primary Drive:	Chain	Chain	Helical Gear
Ignition & Lights:	Magneto, 6volt-20Watt	Magneto, 6V. - 20W.	Magneto, 6V. - 23W.
Gear Ratios: 1st	28.39:1	28.39:1	15.22:1
2nd	15.21:1	15.21:1	9.55:1
3rd	10.28:1	10.28:1	6.64:1
4th	-	-	5.30:1
Final Drive Ratio:	7.92:1	4.61:1	57:1
Tires:(Pirelli)	front-3.00 x 10	front - 2¼ x 16	front - 3.00 x 10
	rear - 3.50 x 10	rear - 2¼ x 16	rear - 3.00 x 10
Suspension: front:	Telescopic Fork	Telescopic Fork	Telescopic Fork
rear:	Swing Arm w/Damper	Swing Arm w/Damper	Swing Arm w/Damper
Weight:(Dry)	106 lbs.	99 lbs.	105 lbs.
Wheelbase:	42 in.	41 in.	38 in.
Ground Clearance:	7 in.	6 in.	6 in.
Foot Peg Height:	9 in.	9.5 in.	8 in.
Seat Height:	28 in.	25 in.	27 in.
Top Speed:	45 m.p.h.	50 m.p.h.	50 m.p.h.
Colors Availible:	Red, Metallic Gold	Red & White,	Metallic Red,
		Blue & White	Metallic Blue

INDIAN-CLYMER MOTORCYCLE DIVISION	GROUP FRAME Refer to: (Photo No. 23 Page No. 54)	Page No. 51

Part number	No. Pcs.	DESCRIPTION
11200	1	Frame
11201	1	Side stand
618	1	Spring
11202	1	Rear fork
11204	1	Curved tube
2105	2	Bush nylon
2104	1	Pivot TE 12MBx156
10501	1	Front fork complete
10401/1	1	Fork body
10501/1	1	R.H. fork leg
10501/2	1	L.H. fork leg
10401/4	1	Plate
10401/5	2	Rubber
10401/6	2	Spring
10401/7	2	Bush nylon below
10401/8	2	Upper bush nylon
10006/6	2	Felt
10401/9	2	Plate
10006/8	2	Plate
10006/10	2	Pin
10006/11	2	Nut 8MA
10006/12	2	Washer
10401/10	2	Nut 8MA
10401/11	4	Inner washer
11104	1	Front fender
11221	1	Rear fender
10504	2	Front fender bracket
10256	2	Rear shock absorber mm. 290
602/21	4	Spacer
11205	1	Seat
608	1	Outer upper steering column bearing
609	1	Outer lower steering column bearing

INDIAN-CLYMER MOTORCYCLE DIVISION	**GROUP FRAME** Refer to: (Photo No. 23 Page No. 54)	Page No 52

Part number	No. Pcs.	DESCRIPTION
610	1	Inner upper steering column bearing
611	1	Inner lower steering column bearing
613	1	Nut
613/1	2	Washer
612	52	Ball bearing
11206	1	Chain guard
641	1	R.H. foot rest
642	1	L.H. foot rest
8033	2	Foot rest rubber
848	1	Couple chain stretcher
11207	1	Engine
11207/1	1	Kick starter lever
601/3	1	Gear change lever complete
2039	1	Head engine connection
2040	1	Silentblock
11208	1	Fuel tank
10042	1	Fuel tank plug
652	1	Fuel cock one way
633	1	Fuel cock two way
634	5	Fuel cock gasket
3103	1	Tool box
3103/1	1	Ball grip
11209	1	Fuel connection between cocks
11209/1	1	Fuel connection between cock-carburettor
11210	1	Couple "Indian" gold decalco
11211	1	PAPOOSE decalco
12226	1	"Designed by Tartarini" decalco
1307	1	Exhaust pipe with muffler
10255	1	Muffler cover
697	4	Shock-absorber spacer
2019	1	Tool bag
11222	2	Rubber ring

INDIAN-CLYMER MOTORCYCLE DIVISION		GROUP FRAME Refer to: (Photo No. 23 Page No. 54)	Page No. 53
Part number	No. Pcs.	DESCRIPTION	
11219	2	Tool box rest	
653	1	Rubber	

page n. 54

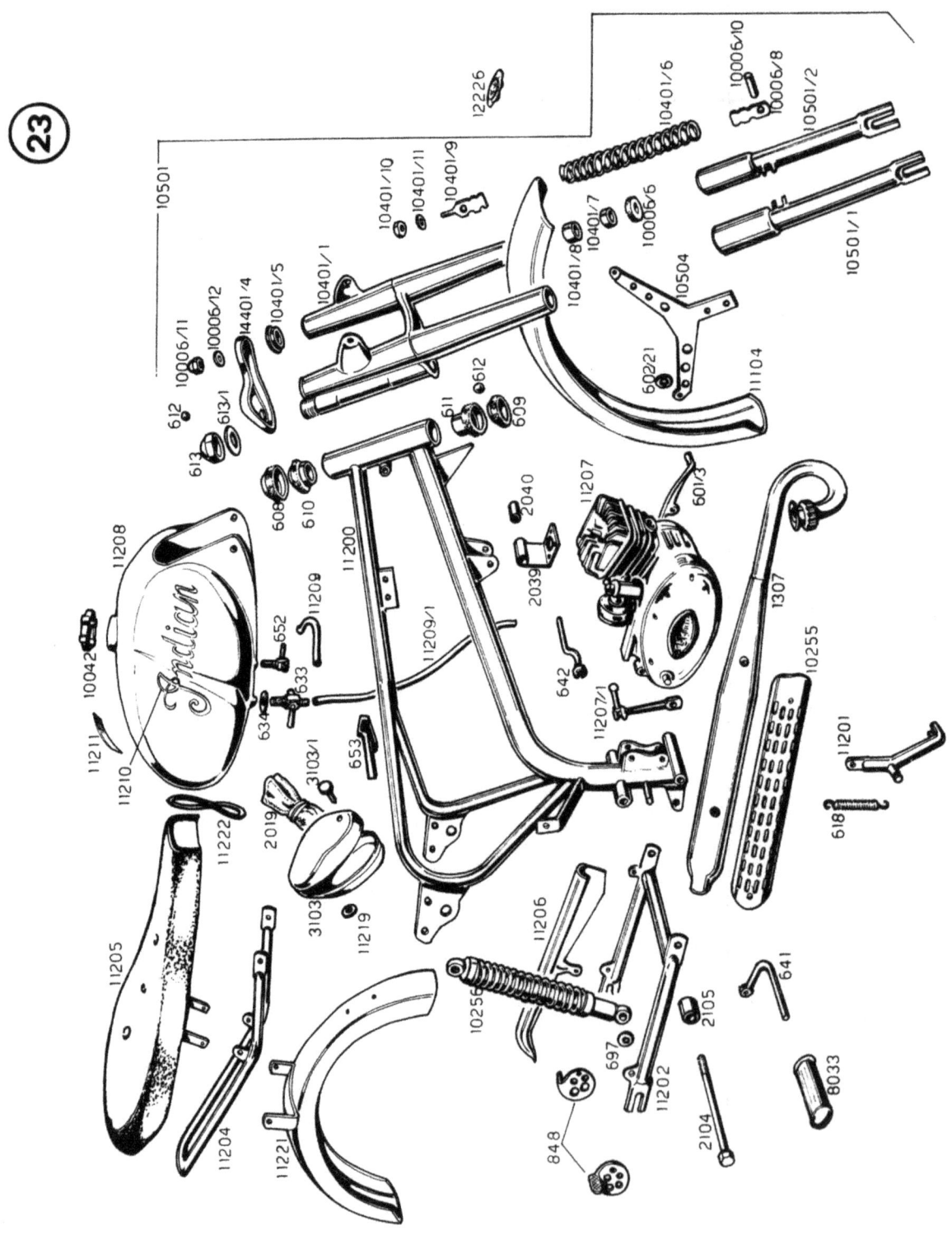

INDIAN-CLYMER MOTORCYCLE DIVISION	GROUP CONTROLS AND WHEELS	Page No 55
	Refer to: (Photo No. 24 Page No. 59)	

Part number	No. Pcs.	DESCRIPTION
11212	1	Handle bar
1439	1	Couple little forks fixing handle bar
10250	1	Gas control
1427	1	R.H. lever
1428	1	L.H. lever
1427/1	1	Front brake lever
1427/2	1	Front brake lever rest
1428/1	1	L.H. clutch lever
1428/2	1	Clutch lever rest
660/3	2	Screw
10253/5	2	Screw
10228	1	R.H. handle
10229	1	L.H. handle
659	2	Hold-fast
11214	1	Wire gas control
11213	1	Wire clutch control
10218/2	1	Wire front brake control
11215	1	Wire rear brake control
667/1	1	Hold-fast
670	1	Little fork with pin
667/2	1	Tender
10026	1	Front tire 3.00 - 10
10027	1	Rear tire 3.50 - 10
10043	1	Front tube 9A 10
10044	1	Rear tube 12A 10
10028	2	Flaps
10413	1	Front wheel complete
10221	1	Rear wheel complete
10413/1	1	Front hub complete
10413/2	1	Front hub body
10413/3	1	Pin
10035/3	4	Cap

INDIAN-CLYMER MOTORCYCLE DIVISION	**GROUP** CONTROLS AND WHEELS Refer to: (Photo No. 24 Page No. 59)	Page No. 56

Part number	No. Pcs.	DESCRIPTION
10035/4	4	Cone
10035/5	4	Dust cover
10036/6	4	Nut
681/7	40	Ball
682/9	4	Nut
10413/6	1	Spacer h. 3
10413/4	1	Spacer h. 6
682/15	4	Washer
10036/3	2	Pairs of shoes with sole
10036/4	4	Spring
10036/5	2	Spinner
10036/6	2	Nut
10036/7	2	Washer
10036/8	2	Lever
10413/5	1	Cover
681/12	1	Adjuster
681/18	2	Clamp with nut and washer
10036	1	Rear hub complete
10036/1	1	Rear hub body
10036/2	1	Pin
10036/9	1	Cover
10036/10	1	Spacer h. 14
10035/7	1	Spacer
677	1	Plate
12221/4	2	Nut
682/13	4	Bolt fixing sprocket
682/14	4	Nut
10221/3	1	Adjuster
10221/1	1	Sprocket 22T.
10032	2	Steel rim 10x54
10033	56	Nipples
10034	28	Front spoke ⌀ 2,5

INDIAN-CLYMER MOTORCYCLE DIVISION	GROUP CONTROLS AND WHEELS Refer to: (Photo No. 24 Page No. 59)	Page No 57

Part number	No. Pcs.	DESCRIPTION
10221/2	28	Rear spoke ø 3
10030	1	Spring
8121	1	Spring
11203	1	Rear brake lever
11216	1	Chain T.54 83 links
684/1	5	Clip
684	5	Long clip
11217	1	Cables assembly
10039	1	Light switch
985/1	1	Coil cable
10052	1	Head lamp complete ø 105
10052/1	1	Head lamp body
10052/2	1	Head lamp ring screw
10052/3	1	Optical set
10052/4	12	Spring
10010/1	1	Cable
10053	1	Tail lamp with plate holder
10053/1	1	Tail lamp body
10053/2	1	Plate holder
10053/3	1	Rear lamp glass
10053/4	1	Bulb
10053/5	1	Rubber
10053/6	1	Gasket
10053/7	1	Cap
10053/8	1	Glass for illumination plate
10053/9	2	Screw
10053/10	2	Nut
10053/11	2	Washer
1013	1	Stop switch
11218	1	Pawl
10068	1	Plug pipe
11220	1	Hold-fast

INDIAN-CLYMER MOTORCYCLE DIVISION	GROUP CONTROLS AND WHEELS	Page No 58
	Refer to: (Photo No. 24 Page No. 30)	

Part number	No. Pcs.	DESCRIPTION
10225	1	Horn 6V. 18W.
1420/2	1	Outer ignition coil
1015	1	Plug pipe
693	2	Cables guard
11116	1	Complete speedometer set
11116/1	1	Speedometer body
10227/1	1	L.H. speedometer drive
10412/1	1	Complete cable
10412/3	1	Housing cable
10412/4	1	Inner cable
3115	1	Ring
690	2	Rubber cable way
670/1	1	Little fork

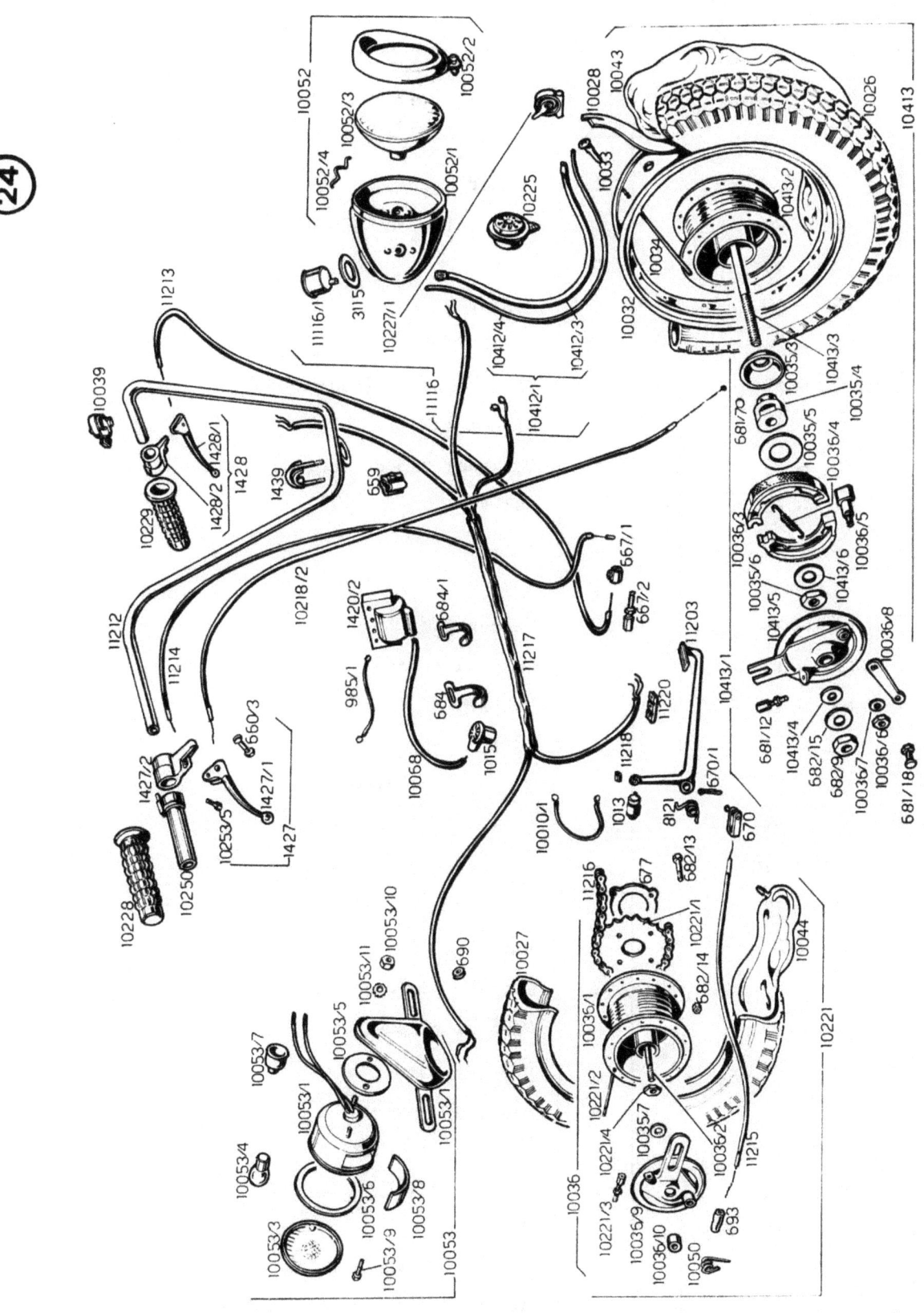

INDIAN-CLYMER MOTORCYCLE DIVISION	**GROUP** HEAD CYLINDER AND GEAR-BOX P4S ASSEMBLY Refer to: (Photo No. 25 Page No. 62)		Page No 60

Refer. No.	Part number	No. Pcs.	DESCRIPTION
1	—	1	Filter F.26/5
2	M24 - 24	1	Carburettor UA 19S without filter
3	M24 - 16	1	Pipe
4	M38 - 39	1	Gasket
5	M2 - 25	1	Spark plug CW 240
6	M24 - 12	1	Head "sport" (square)
7	M2 - 11	1	Gasket
8	M24 - 13	1	Cylinder "Sport" bore 38,8
9	M6 - 11	1	Gasket
10	M6 - 10	1	Ring
11	C2 - 17	4	Nut
12	M1 - 33	4	Washer ⌀ 6
13	M2 - 13	4	Fastening screw
14	M2 - 10	1	Gasket
15	A24 - 7	2	Piston ring ⌀ 38,8x1,5x1,5
15	A24 - 7M	2	Piston ring over 2-4-6-8/10
16	A24 - 31	1	Piston ⌀ 38,8 "Sport"
16	A24 - 31M	1	Piston over 2-4-6-8/10
17	A24 - 15	1	Connecting rod ⌀ 22
18	A2 - 8	1	Bush
19	A2 - 9	1	Gudgeon pin ⌀ 12x31,5
20	A2 - 10	2	Wire circlip
21	A2 - 20	1	Ring 17-35-8
22	C1 - 17	1	Bearing 17-40-12 (RIV.01A)
23	A24 - 12	1	R.H. crank shaft
24	A24 - 14	1	Cage 16-22-12
25	A24 - 13	1	Pin ⌀ 16
26	A24 - 11	1	R.H. crank shaft ⌀ 16
27	A2 - 19	1	Bearing 15-35-11 (RIV.02A)
28	A2 - 21	1	Ring 15-30-8
29	A1 - 25	1	Little key for flywheel
30	A2 - 16	1	Little key for sprocket

INDIAN-CLYMER MOTORCYCLE DIVISION	GROUP HEAD CYLINDER AND GEAR-BOX P4S ASSEMBLY Refer to: (Photo No. 25 Page No. 62)	Page No 61

Refer. No.	Part number	No. Pcs.	DESCRIPTION
31	C42 - 10	1	Bush
32	C1 - 16	1	Washer ∅ 13
33	C42 - 2	1	Primary shaft
34	A2 - 19	1	Bearing 15-35-11 (RIV. 02A)
35	C2 - 11	1	Ring 15-24-5
36	C2 - 23	1	Washer ∅ 35
37	A2 - 19	1	Bearing 15-35-11 (RIV. 02A)
38	C2 - 9	1	Washer ∅ 15
39	C2 - 8	1	Seeger ∅ 15
40	C2 - 9	1	Washer ∅ 15
41	C42 - 3	1	Secondary shaft
42	C42 - 9	1	4th gear 23T.
43	C42 - 8	1	Disk operating 3rd and 4th gear
44	C42 - 7	1	3rd gear 26T.
45	A20 - 7	1	Washer
46	C42 - 6	1	2nd gear 29T.
47	C15 - 9	2	Ring ∅ 16
48	C42 - 5	1	Disk operating 1st and 2nd gear
49	C42 - 4	1	1st gear 33T.
50	C1 - 16	1	Washer ∅ 13
51	C5 - 19	1	Bush ∅ 13x13
52	M3 - 17	2	Screw TE 6MAx20
53	M1 - 33	2	Washer ∅ 6
54	U42 - 1	-	Crankshaft puller
55	A24 - 16	1	Complete connecting rod
56	A24 - 10	1	Complete crankshaft
57	C42 - 1	1	Complete gear-box
58	M32 - 17	4	Bolt

page n. 62

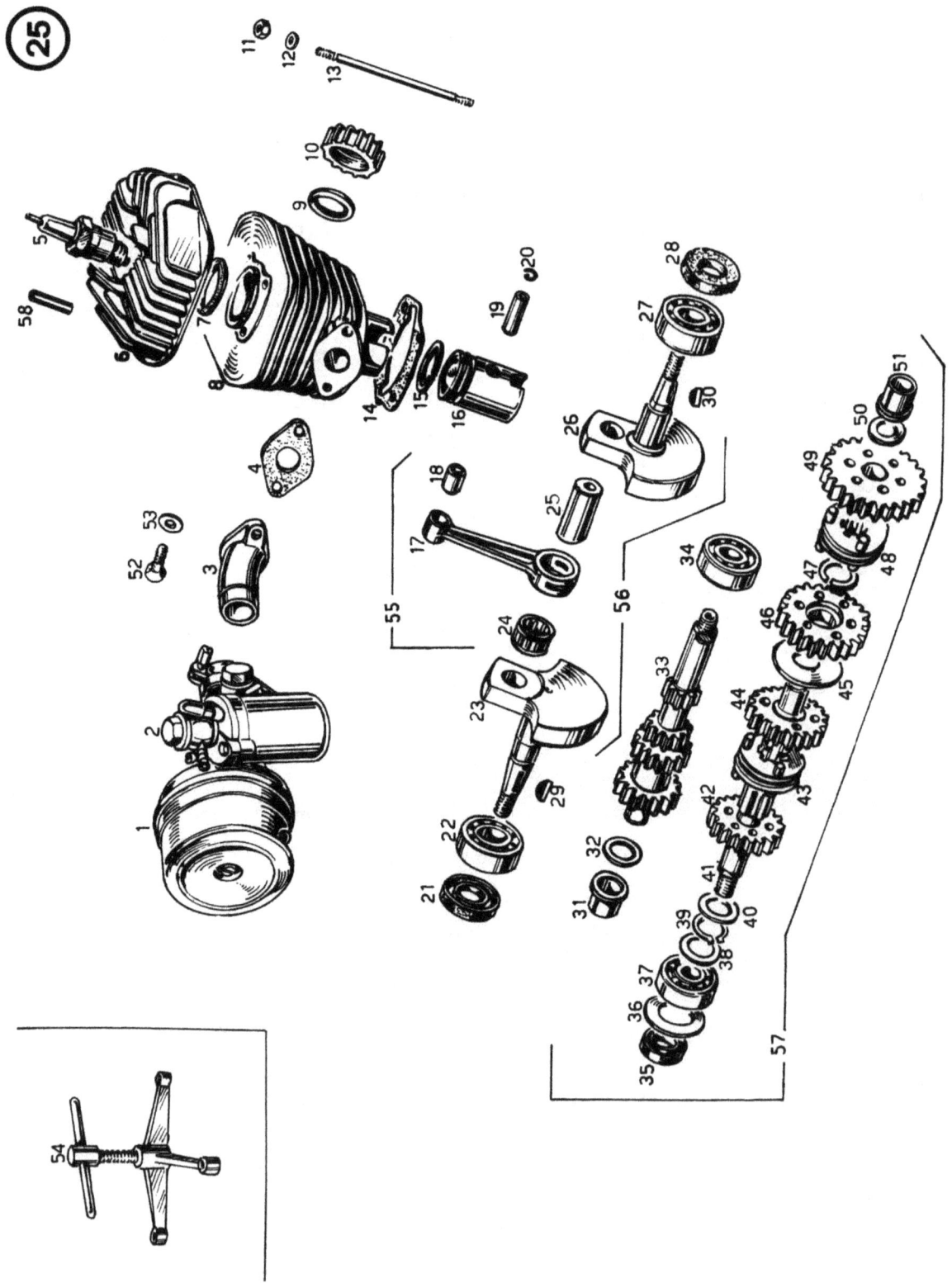

| | INDIAN-CLYMER MOTORCYCLE DIVISION | GROUP CLUTCH CRANKCASE P4C ASSEMBLY Refer to: (Photo No. 26   Page No. 65) | Page No 53 |

Refer. No.	Part number	No. Pcs.	DESCRIPTION
1	F42 - 4	1	Clutch lever
2	F38 - 11	1	Spring
3	F42 - 1	1	Clutch operating rod
4	S1 - 7	1	Ring
5	F42 - 2	1	Bolt
6	F2 - 21	1	Ball 3/16"
7	F2 - 13	1	Washer
8	F2 - 14	1	Nut 9 11
9	F1 - 20	1	Pusher clutch disk
10	M42 - 1	1	Half crankcase
11	M5 - 25	1	Plug
12	M5 - 26	2	Gasket
13	M42 - 4	1	Gasket
14	C1 - 22	1	Washer Ø 12
15	F2 - 16	6	Rivet
16	A42 - 1	1	Engine sprocket
17	A2 - 14	1	Washer
18	A42 - 2	1	Nut
19	F2 - 12	4	Ring
20	F2 - 10	4	Clutch spring
21	F2 - 11	4	Screw
22	M42 - 5	1	Gasket
23	M42 - 3	1	Clutch cover
24	M1 - 38	5	Screw TE 6MMx35
25	M2 - 12	1	Gasket
26	M2 - 7	1	"Minarelli" plate
27	M2 - 26	2	Screw T.G.S. 4MMx10
28	M2 - 9	1	Gasket Ø 6
29	M2 - 8	1	Screw oil level 6MM
30	F38 - 1	1	Clutch gear 60T.
31	C2 - 9	2	Washer Ø 15
32	F2 - 3	1	Steel plate

	INDIAN-CLYMER MOTORCYCLE DIVISION	GROUP CLUTCH CRANKCASE P4S ASSEMBLY Refer to: (Photo No. 26 Page No. 65)	Page No 64

Refer. No.	Part number	No. Pcs.	DESCRIPTION
33	F2 - 6	3	Steel plate ∅ 1,3
34	F38 - 10	4	Cork clutch disk ∅ 3,1
35	F2 - 7	1	Plate
36	F2 - 9	1	Nut
37	F2 - 8	1	Screw
38	M42 - 7	1	Plate
39	M42 - 9	3	Washer ∅ 3
40	M42 - 8	3	Screw TC 3MAx5
41	MM42 - 2	1	Kick starter sprocket 23T.
42	MM42 - 5	1	Kick starter gear
43	KS38 - 11	1	Spring
44	MM1 - 9	1	Seeger ∅ 18
45	MM5 - 7	1	Ring
46	MM42 - 4	1	Spring
47	M1 - 36	6	Screw TC 6Mx25
48	MM42 - 1	1	Kick starter shaft
49	MM1 - 10	1	Ring ST. 317
50	MM42 - 3	1	Screw
51	MM1 - 5	1	Washer
52	F2 - 20	1	Screw
53	U2 - 1	-	Puller
54	U2 - 4	-	Engine sprocket puller
55	U2 - 6	-	Key
56	U2 - 11	-	Key
57	F2 - 2	1	Clutch bell

page n. 65

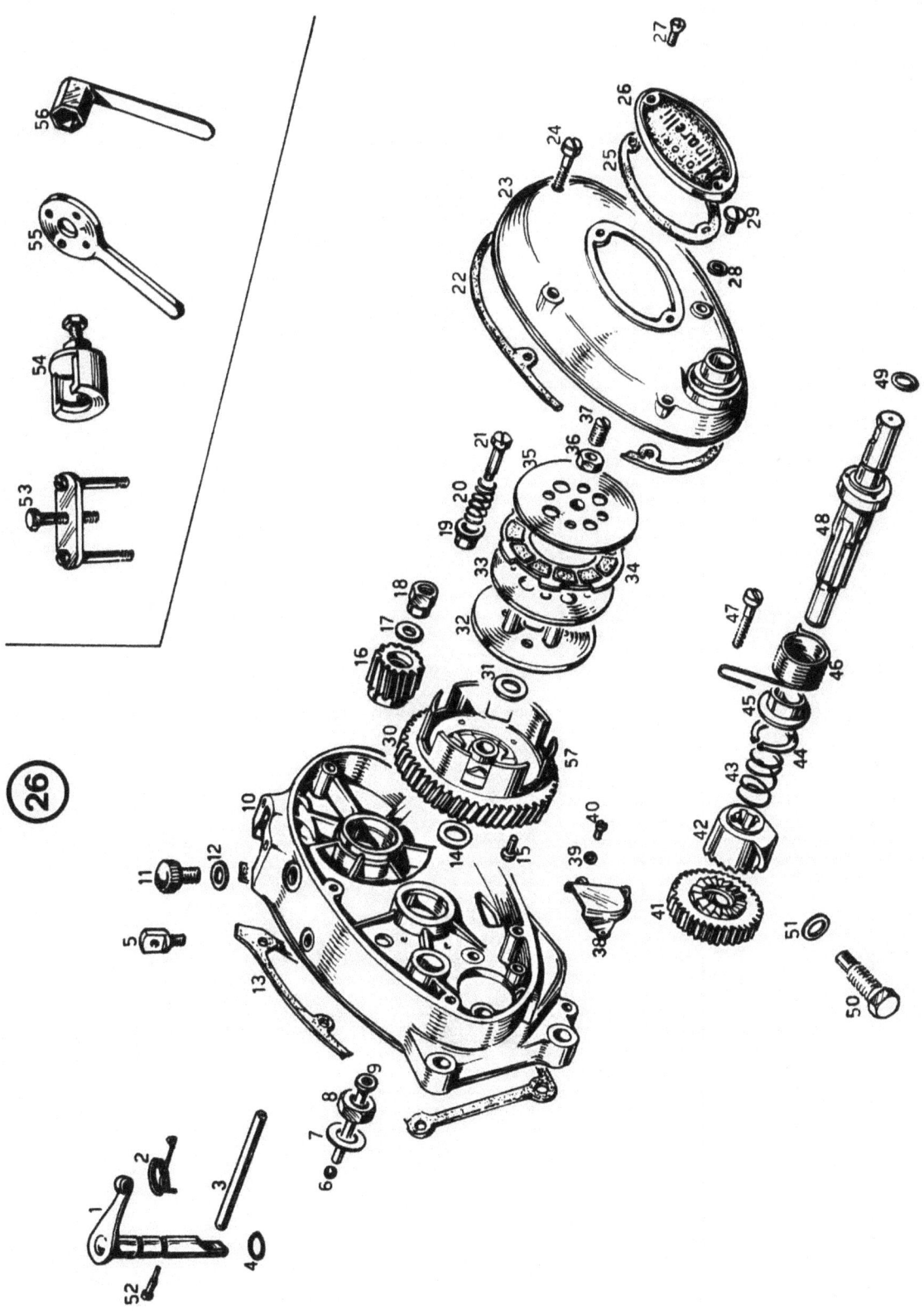

| INDIAN-CLYMER MOTORCYCLE DIVISION | GROUP: CRANKCASE - KICK STARTER GEARS AND FLYWHEEL ASSEMBLY Refer to: (Photo No. 27   Page No. 69) | Page No. 66 |

Refer. No.	Part number	No. Pcs.	DESCRIPTION
1	M2 - 26	2	Screw T.G.S. 4MAx10
2	M2 - 7	1	"Minarelli" plate
3	M1 - 37	2	Screw TC 6MAx30
4	M38 - 4	1	Flywheel cover
5	A2 - 17	1	Nut
6	A1 - 27	3	Screw
7	M38 - 48	1	Complete flywheel 6V. 23W.
8	V31 - 1	1	Inductor group
8A	V20 - 8	1	Coil rest
9-13	V2 - 2	2	Screw and washer
10	V2 - 4	1	Screw
11	V2 - 5	1	Cam
12-17	V2 - 3	2	Screw and washer
14	V2 - 7	1	Contact breaker
15	V31 - 3	1	Rotor
16	V2 - 10	1	Felt
18	V2 - 13	1	Rotor BT
19	V2 - 9	1	Screw
20	V2 - 12	1	Condenser
21	V2 - 14	1	Plate for rotors
			When ordering flywheel parts, please remember to specify the number and the mark of Inductor.-
22	C2 - 24	1	Nut
23	C2 - 25	1	Washer ∅ 10
24	C2 - 12	1	Sprocket 14T.
25	M4 - 25	1	Screw 6MAx40
26	M1 - 40	2	Screw TC. 6MAx50
27	M42 - 2	1	Half crankcase
28	M29 - 16	2	Pin ∅ 10x30
29	M7 - 14	1	Screw TC. 6MAx65
30	M1 - 36	6	Screw TC. 6MAx25
31	M2 - 33	2	Screw TC. 6MAx20

| INDIAN-CLYMER MOTORCYCLE DIVISION | GROUP CRANKCASE – KICK STARTER GEARS AND FLYWHEEL ASSEMBLY Refer to: (Photo No. 27 Page No. 69) | Page No 67 |

Refer. No.	Part number	No. Pcs.	DESCRIPTION
32	S1 – 18	1	Gasket ∅ 8
33	S5 – 27	1	Screw
34	S42 – 13	1	Pin
35	S42 – 10	1	Plate
36	S4 – 21	1	Washer ∅ 10
37	S42 – 1	1	Cams
38	S42 – 10	1	Plate
39	S42 – 12	1	Pin
40	S42 – 15	1	Washer ∅ 7
41	S1 – 24	1	Nut
42	S4 – 21	1	Washer ∅ 10
43	S4 – 15	1	Ball 5/16"
44	S42 – 17	1	Spring
45	S42 – 3	1	Cup
46	S4 – 18	1	Ring 12-22-7
47	C1 – 22	2	Washer ∅ 12
48	S4 – 22	1	Seeger ∅ 12
49	S42 – 18	1	Washer
50	S42 – 8	1	Spring
51	S42 – 9	1	Washer
52	S42 – 7	1	Plate
53	S42 – 4	1	Shaft operating selector
54	S42 – 6	1	Spring
55	S42 – 14	1	Screw
56	S42 – 15	1	Washer ∅ 7
57	S4 – 5	1	Spring rest
58	C2 – 8	1	Seeger ∅ 15
59	S4 – 21	1	Washer ∅ 10
60	N38 – 21	1	Rubber
61	U2 – 3	–	Sprocket puller
62	U2 – 8	–	Sprocket key
63	U1 – 2	–	Flywheel puller

INDIAN-CLYMER MOTORCYCLE DIVISION	GROUP CRANKCASE - KICK STARTER GEARS AND FLYWHEEL ASSEMBLY Refer to: (Photo No. 27 Page No. 60)	Page No 68

Refer. No.	Part number	No. Pcs.	DESCRIPTION
64	U29 - 1	-	Flywheel key CEV or DUCATI
65	V31 - 5	1	Plate
66	M2 - 24	1	**Rubber**

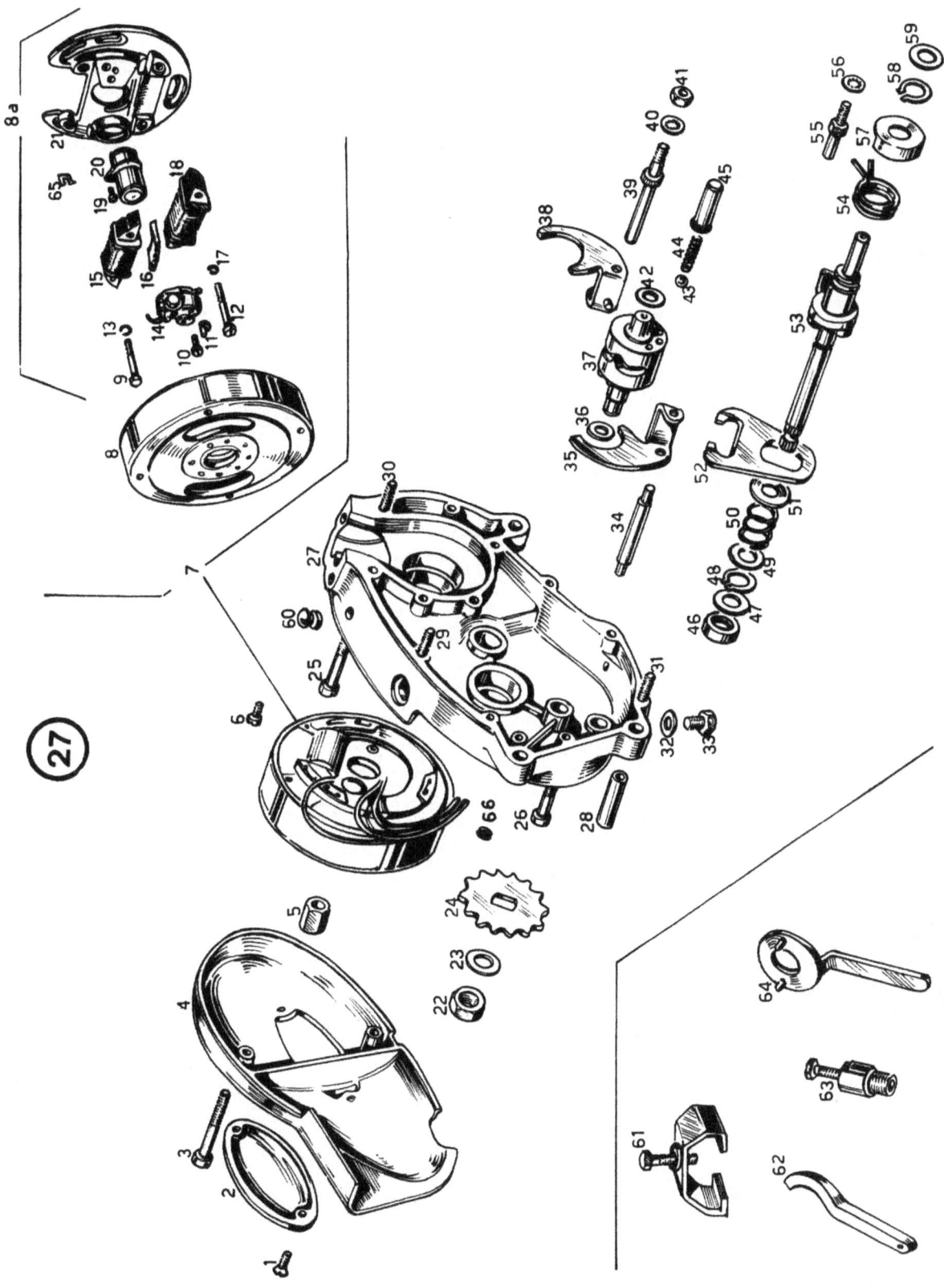

page n. 69

| INDIAN-CLYMER MOTORCYCLE DIVISION | GROUP COMPLETE CARBURETTOR UA 19S Refer to: (Photo No. 28 Page No. 72) | Page No 70 |

Part number	No. Pcs.	DESCRIPTION
----	1	Complete carburettor
1111 - 36	1	Screw
1382 - 30	2	Gasket
1407 - 21	1	Needle circlip
1409 - 61	1	Spring
1410 - 61	1	Spring
1411 - 61	2	Spring
1414 - 30	1	Gasket
1416 - 30	2	Pipe gasket
1419 - 29	1	Fuel filter
4884x64	1	Throttle valve
1423x80	1	Float complete
1425x08	1	Needle
1427 - 60	1	Ring
1452 - 21	1	Ring
1481 - 37	1	Screw
1485x28	1	Jet holder
1486x02	1	Main jet
1488x02	1	Idling jet
1491 - 36	2	Screw
1492 - 25	1	Mixer
1493 - 21	1	Ring
1494 - 34	1	Pipe plug
1532 - 37	1	Screw
1607x05	1	Pin
1642 - 53	1	Cover
1692 - 27	1	Nut
1721 - 50	1	Ring
2063 - 96	1	Float chamber
2086 - 34	1	Plug
2115 - 37	1	Screw
2706 - 38	1	Pipe

INDIAN-CLYMER MOTORCYCLE DIVISION	GROUP COMPLETE CARBURETTOR UA 19S Refer to: (Photo No. 28 Page No. 7?)	Page No 71

Part number	No. Pcs.	DESCRIPTION
3570 - 21	1	Tweezers
4477 - 62	1	Seal ring
1584 - 54	1	Cover
5010 - 23	2	Gasket
10.111	1	Filter F.25/5 complete
4276 - 36	1	Screw
4028 - 85	1	Filter cover
4076 - 35	1	Spacer
4483 - 86	1	Filter
4026 - 30	1	Gasket

GROUP

COMPLETE CARBURETTOR UA 19S

page n. 72

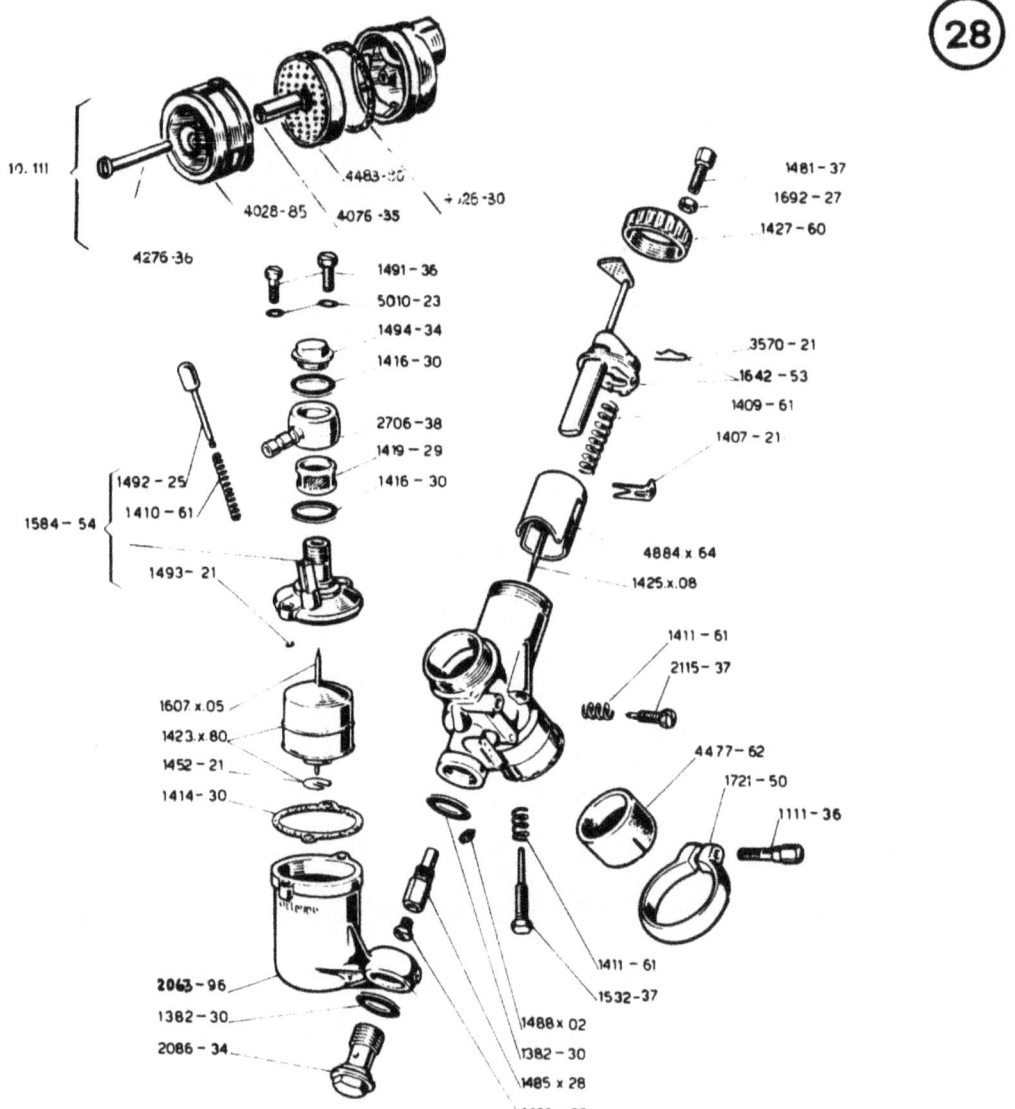

NOTES

ARE YOU:
INTERESTED IN EUROPEAN, IMPORT & EXOTIC AUTOMOBILES?

DO YOU:
DO YOUR OWN MAINTENANCE?

If you answered yes to either of these questions, then you should check out our automobile books and manuals. We have included a sample listing of some of our featured marques. However, for complete details and the most up-to-date information, please visit our website.

—— www.VelocePress.com ——

The fastest growing specialist USA publisher of niche market automotive books and manuals.

All VelocePress titles are available through your local independent bookseller, Amazon.com or direct from VelocePress. Wholesale customers may also purchase direct or from the Ingram Book Group.

AUTOBOOKS WORKSHOP MANUALS

ALFA ROMEO GIULIA 1300, 1600, 1750, 2000 1962-1978 WSM
AUSTIN HEALEY SPRITE, MG MIDGET 1958-1980 WSM
BMW 1600 1966-1973 WSM
BMW 2000 & 2002 1966-1976 WSM
BMW 2500, 2800, 3.0 & 3.3 1968-1977 WSM
BMW 316, 320, 320i 1975-1977 WSM
BMW 518, 520, 520i 1973-1981 WSM
FIAT 1100, 1100D, 1100R & 1200 1957-1969 WSM
FIAT 124 1966-1974 WSM
FIAT 124 SPORT 1966-1975 WSM
FIAT 125 & 125 SPECIAL 1967-1973 WSM
FIAT 126, 126L, 126 DV, 126/650 & 126/650 DV 1972-1982 WSM
FIAT 127 SALOON, SPECIAL & SPORT, 900, 1050 1971-1981 WSM
FIAT 128 1969-1982 WSM
FIAT 1300, 1500 1961-1967 WSM
FIAT 131 MIRAFIORI 1975-1982 WSM
FIAT 132 1972-1982 WSM
FIAT 500 1957-1973 WSM
FIAT 600, 600D & MULTIPLA 1955-1969 WSM
FIAT 850 1964-1972 WSM
JAGUAR E-TYPE 1961-1972 WSM
JAGUAR MK 1, 2 1955-1969 WSM
JAGUAR S TYPE, 420 1963-1968 WSM
JAGUAR XK 120, 140, 150 MK 7, 8, 9 1948-1961 WSM
LAND ROVER 1, 2 1948-1961 WSM
MERCEDES-BENZ 190 1959-1968 WSM
MERCEDES-BENZ 220/8 1968-1972 WSM
MERCEDES-BENZ 220B 1959-1965 WSM
MERCEDES-BENZ 230 1963-1968 WSM
MERCEDES-BENZ 250 1968-1972 WSM
MERCEDES-BENZ 280 1968-1972 WSM
MG MIDGET TA-TF 1936-1955 WSM
MINI 1959-1980 WSM
MORRIS MINOR 1952-1971 WSM
PEUGEOT 404 1960-1975 WSM
PORSCHE 911 1964-1973 WSM
PORSCHE 911 1970-1977 WSM
RENAULT 16 1965-1979 WSM
RENAULT 8, 10, 1100 1962-1971 WSM
ROVER 3500, 3500S 1968-1976 WSM
SUNBEAM RAPIER, ALPINE 1955-1965 WSM
TRIUMPH SPITFIRE, GT6, VITESSE 1962-1968 WSM
TRIUMPH TR2, TR3, TR3A 1952-1962 WSM
TRIUMPH TR4, TR4A 1961-1967 WSM
VOLKSWAGEN BEETLE 1968-1977 WSM

BROOKLANDS BOOKS & ROAD TEST PORTFOLIOS (RTP)

AC CARS 1904-2009
ALFA ROMEO 1920-1933 ROAD TEST PORTFOLIO
ALFA ROMEO 1934-1940 ROAD TEST PORTFOLIO
BRABHAM RALT HONDA THE RON TAURANAC STORY
BUGATTI TYPE 10 TO TYPE 40 ROAD TEST PORTFOLIO
BUGATTI TYPE 10 TO TYPE 251 ROAD TEST PORTFOLIO
BUGATTI TYPE 41 TO TYPE 55 ROAD TEST PORTFOLIO
BUGATTI TYPE 57 TO TYPE 251 ROAD TEST PORTFOLIO
DELAHAYE ROAD TEST PORTFOLIO
FERRARI ROAD CARS 1946-1956 ROAD TEST PORTFOLIO
FIAT 500 1936-1972 ROAD TEST PORTFOLIO
FIAT DINO ROAD TEST PORTFOLIO
HISPANO SUIZA ROAD TEST PORTFOLIO
HONDA ST1100/ST1300 PAN EUROPEAN 1990-2002 RTP
JAGUAR MK1 & MK2 ROAD TEST PORTFOLIO
LOTUS CORTINA ROAD TEST PORTFOLIO
MV AGUSTA F4 750 & 1000 1997-2007 ROAD TEST PORTFOLIO
TATRA CARS ROAD TEST PORTFOLIO

VELOCEPRESS AUTOMOBILE BOOKS & MANUALS

ABARTH BUYERS GUIDE
AUSTIN-HEALEY 6-CYLINDER WSM
BMW 600 LIMOUSINE FACTORY WSM
BMW 600 LIMOUSINE OWNERS HAND BOOK & SERVICE MANUAL
BMW ISETTA FACTORY WSM
BOOK OF THE CARRERA PANAMERICANA - MEXICAN ROAD RACE
COMPLETE CATALOG OF JAPANESE MOTOR VEHICLES
DIALED IN - THE JAN OPPERMAN STORY
FERRARI 250/GT SERVICE AND MAINTENANCE
FERRARI 308 SERIES BUYER'S AND OWNER'S GUIDE
FERRARI BERLINETTA LUSSO
FERRARI BROCHURES AND SALES LITERATURE 1946-1967
FERRARI BROCHURES AND SALES LITERATURE 1968-1989
FERRARI GUIDE TO PERFORMANCE
FERRARI OPP, MAINTENANCE & SERVICE H/BOOKS 1948-1963
FERRARI OWNER'S HANDBOOK
FERRARI SERIAL NUMBERS PART I - ODD NUMBERS TO 21399
FERRARI SERIAL NUMBERS PART II - EVEN NUMBERS TO 1050
FERRARI SPYDER CALIFORNIA
FERRARI TUNING TIPS & MAINTENANCE TECHNIQUES
HENRY'S FABULOUS MODEL "A" FORD
HOW TO BUILD A FIBERGLASS CAR
HOW TO BUILD A RACING CAR
IF HEMINGWAY HAD WRITTEN A RACING NOVEL
JAGUAR E-TYPE 3.8 & 4.2 WSM
LE MANS 24 (THE BOOK THAT THE FILM WAS BASED ON)
MASERATI BROCHURES AND SALES LITERATURE
MASERATI OWNER'S HANDBOOK
METROPOLITAN FACTORY WSM
MGA & MGB OWNERS HANDBOOK & WSM
OBERT'S FIAT GUIDE
PERFORMANCE TUNING THE SUNBEAM TIGER
PORSCHE 356 1948-1965 WSM
PORSCHE 912 WSM
SOUPING THE VOLKSWAGEN
TRIUMPH TR2, TR3, TR4 1953-1965 WSM
VEDA ORR'S NEW REVISED HOT ROD PICTORIAL
VOLKSWAGEN TRANSPORTER, TRUCKS, STATION WAGONS WSM
VOLVO 1944-1968 ALL MODELS WSM

VELOCEPRESS MOTORCYCLE BOOKS & MANUALS

AJS SINGLES 1955-65 350cc & 500cc (BOOK OF)
ARIEL 1939-1960 4 STROKE SINGLES (BOOK OF)
ARIEL LEADER & ARROW 1958-1964 (BOOK OF)
ARIEL MOTORCYCLES 1933-1951 WSM
ARIEL PREWAR MODELS 1932-1939 (BOOK OF)
BMW M/CYCLES R26 R27 (1956-1967) FACTORY WSM
BMW M/CYCLES R50 R50S R60 R69S (1955-1969) FACTORY WSM
BSA BANTAM (BOOK OF)
BSA ALL FOUR-STROKE SINGLES & V-TWINS 1936-1952 (BOOK OF)
BSA OHV & SV SINGLES - 250cc 1954-1970 (BOOK OF)
BSA OHV & SV SINGLES 1945-54 250-600cc (BOOK OF)
BSA OHV SINGLES 350 & 500cc 1955-1967 (BOOK OF)
BSA PRE-WAR MODELS TO 1939 (BOOK OF)
BSA TWINS 1948-1962 (BOOK OF)
BSA TWINS 1962-1969 (SECOND BOOK OF)
CATALOG OF BRITISH MOTORCYCLES (1951 MODELS)
DOUGLAS PRE-WAR ALL MODELS 1929-1939 (BOOK OF)
DOUGLAS POST-WAR ALL MODELS 1948-1957 FACTORY WSM
DUCATI 160cc, 250cc & 350cc OHC MODELS FACTORY WSM
HONDA 50 ALL MODELS UP TO 1970 INC MONKEY & TRAIL (BOOK OF)
HONDA 90 ALL MODELS UP TO 1966 (BOOK OF)
HONDA MOTORCYCLES 125-150 TWINS C/CS/CB/CA WSM
HONDA MOTORCYCLES 250-305 TWINS C/CS/CB WSM
HONDA MOTORCYCLES C100 SUPER CUB WSM
HONDA MOTORCYCLES C110 SPORT CUB 1962-1969 WSM
HONDA TWINS & SINGLES 50cc TO 305cc 1960-1966 (BOOK OF)
HONDA TWINS ALL MODELS 125cc THRU 450cc UP TO 1968 (BOOK OF)
INDIAN PONYBIKE, BOY RACER & PAPOOSE ILLUSTRATED PARTS LIST
LAMBRETTA ALL 125 & 150cc MODELS 1947-1957 (BOOK OF)
LAMBRETTA LI & TV MODELS 1957-1970 (SECOND BOOK OF)
MATCHLESS 350 & 500cc SINGLES 1945-1956 (BOOK OF)
MATCHLESS 350 & 500cc SINGLES 1955-1966 (BOOK OF)
NORTON 1938-1956 (BOOK OF)
NORTON DOMINATOR TWINS 1955-1965 (BOOK OF)
NORTON MOTORCYCLES 1957-1970 FACTORY WSM
NORTON PREWAR MODELS 1932-1939 (BOOK OF)
ROYAL ENFIELD 736cc INTERCEPTOR FACTORY WSM
ROYAL ENFIELD 250cc & 350cc SINGLES 1958-1966 (SECOND BOOK OF)
SUZUKI 50cc & 80cc UP TO 1966 (BOOK OF)
SUZUKI T10 1963-1967 FACTORY WSM
SUZUKI T20 & T200 1965-1969 FACTORY WSM
TRIUMPH PRE-WAR MOTORCYCLE 1935-1939 (BOOK OF)
TRIUMPH MOTORCYCLES 1937-1951 WSM
TRIUMPH MOTORCYCLES 1945-1955 FACTORY WSM
TRIUMPH TWINS 1956-1969 (BOOK OF)
VELOCETTE ALL SINGLES & TWINS 1925-1970 (BOOK OF)
VESPA 1951-1961 (BOOK OF)
VINCENT MOTORCYCLES 1935-1955 WSM

www.VelocePress.com

www.ingramcontent.com/pod-product-compliance
Lightning Source LLC
Chambersburg PA
CBHW080924170426
43201CB00016B/2252